LAW, CRIME AND LAW ENFORCEMENT

ADULT DRUG COURTS

BRIEF OVERVIEW AND ASSESSMENTS

LAW, CRIME AND LAW ENFORCEMENT

Additional books in this series can be found on Nova's website under the Series tab.

Additional e-books in this series can be found on Nova's website under the e-books tab.

LAW, CRIME AND LAW ENFORCEMENT

ADULT DRUG COURTS

BRIEF OVERVIEW AND ASSESSMENTS

JOAN B. CALAHAN
EDITOR

nova publishers
New York

For permission to use material from this book please contact us:
Telephone 631-231-7269; Fax 631-231-8175
Web Site: http://www.novapublishers.com

Library of Congress Cataloging-in-Publication Data

ISBN: 978-1-62417-163-5

Published by Nova Science Publishers, Inc. † New York

CONTENTS

PREFACE

Drug court programs were established beginning in the late 1980s as a local response to increasing numbers of drug-related cases and expanding jail and prison populations nationwide. A drug court is a specialized court-based program that targets criminal offenders who have alcohol and other drug addiction and dependency problems. Drug courts have implemented deferred prosecution or post-adjudication case-processing approaches, or have blended both in their organizational structures. In drug courts, using deferred prosecution, defendants waive rights to a trial and enter a treatment program shortly after being charged; those who subsequently fail to complete the treatment program have their charges adjudicated, while those who complete the program are not prosecuted further. This book provides an overview and assessment of the adult drug court system, with a focus on the rate of recidivism and performance measure revision efforts.

Chapter 1 – A drug court is a specialized court that targets criminal offenders who have drug addiction and dependency problems. These programs provide offenders with intensive court supervision, mandatory drug testing, substance-abuse treatment, and other social services as an alternative to adjudication or incarceration. As of June 2010, there were over 2,500 drug courts operating nationwide, of which about 1,400 target adult offenders. The Department of Justice's (DOJ) Bureau of Justice Assistance (BJA) administers the Adult Drug Court Discretionary Grant Program, which provides financial and technical assistance to develop and implement adult drug-court programs. DOJ requires grantees that receive funding to provide data that measure their performance. In response to the Fair Sentencing Act of 2010, this report assesses (1) data DOJ collected on the performance of federally funded adult drug courts and to what extent DOJ used these data in making grant- related decisions, and (2) what is known about the effectiveness of drug courts. GAO assessed performance data DOJ collected in fiscal year 2010 and reviewed evaluations of 32 drug- court programs and 11 cost-benefit studies issued from February 2004 through March 2011.

Chapter 2 – Drug courts are specialized court docket programs that target criminal defendants and offenders, juvenile offenders, and parents with pending child welfare cases who have alcohol and other drug dependency problems. Although drug courts vary in target population and resources, programs are generally managed by a multidisciplinary team including judges, prosecutors, defense attorneys, community corrections, social workers and treatment service professionals. Support from stakeholders representing law enforcement, the family and the community is encouraged through participation in hearings, programming and events like graduation.

Adult drug courts employ a program designed to reduce drug use relapse and criminal recidivism among defendants and offenders through risk and needs assessment, judicial interaction, monitoring and supervision, graduated sanctions and incentives, treatment and various rehabilitation services.

Chapter 3 - The mission of drug courts is to stop the abuse of alcohol and other drugs and related criminal activity. Drug courts promote recovery through a coordinated response to offenders dependent on alcohol and other drugs. Realization of these goals requires a team approach, including cooperation and collaboration of the judges, prosecutors, defense counsel, probation authorities, other corrections personnel, law enforcement, pretrial services agencies, TASC programs, evaluators, an array of local service providers, and the greater community. State-level organizations representing AOD issues, law enforcement and criminal justice, vocational rehabilitation, education, and housing also have important roles to play. The combined energies of these individuals and organizations can assist and encourage defendants to accept help that could change their lives.

The criminal justice system has the unique ability to influence a person shortly after a significant triggering event such as arrest, and thus persuade or compel that person to enter and remain in treatment. Research indicates that a person coerced to enter treatment by the criminal justice system is likely to do as well as one who volunteers.

In: Adult Drug Courts
Editor: Joan B. Calahan

ISBN: 978-1-62417-163-5

Chapter 1

ADULT DRUG COURTS: STUDIES SHOW COURTS REDUCE RECIDIVISM, BUT DOJ COULD ENHANCE FUTURE PERFORMANCE MEASURE REVISION EFFORTS*

The United States Government Accountability Office

ABBREVIATIONS

BJA	Bureau of Justice Assistance
DOJ	Department of Justice
GPRA	Government Performance and Results Act
GMS	Grants Management System
MADCE	Multi-Site Adult Drug Court Evaluation
NADCP	National Association of Drug Court Professionals
NIJ	National Institute of Justice
OJP	Office of Justice Programs
PMT	Performance Measurement Tool
SAMHSA	Substance Abuse and Mental Health Services Administration

* This is an edited, reformatted and augmented version of The United States Government Accountability Office publication, Report to Congressional Committees GAO-12-53, dated December 2011.

WHY GAO DID THIS STUDY

A drug court is a specialized court that targets criminal offenders who have drug addiction and dependency problems. These programs provide offenders with intensive court supervision, mandatory drug testing, substance-abuse treatment, and other social services as an alternative to adjudication or incarceration. As of June 2010, there were over 2,500 drug courts operating nationwide, of which about 1,400 target adult offenders. The Department of Justice's (DOJ) Bureau of Justice Assistance (BJA) administers the Adult Drug Court Discretionary Grant Program, which provides financial and technical assistance to develop and implement adult drug-court programs. DOJ requires grantees that receive funding to provide data that measure their performance. In response to the Fair Sentencing Act of 2010, this report assesses (1) data DOJ collected on the performance of federally funded adult drug courts and to what extent DOJ used these data in making grant- related decisions, and (2) what is known about the effectiveness of drug courts. GAO assessed performance data DOJ collected in fiscal year 2010 and reviewed evaluations of 32 drug- court programs and 11 cost-benefit studies issued from February 2004 through March 2011.

WHAT GAO RECOMMENDS

GAO recommends that BJA document key methods used to guide future revisions of its performance measures for the adult drug-court program. DOJ concurred with GAO's recommendation.

WHAT GAO FOUND

BJA collects an array of data on adult drug-court grantees, such as drug-court completion rates, and during the course of GAO's review, began expanding its use of this performance data to inform grant-related decisions, such as allocating resources and setting program priorities. For example, during September 2011, BJA assessed a sample of adult drug-court grantees' performance across a range of variables, using a new process it calls GrantStat. BJA developed recommendations following this assessment and is determining their feasibility.

In addition, in October 2011, BJA finalized revisions to the performance measures on which grantees report. BJA's process of revising its performance measures generally adhered to key practices, such as obtaining stakeholder involvement; however, BJA could improve upon two practices as it continues to assess and revise measures in the future.

First, while BJA plans to assess the reliability of the new measures after the first quarter of grantees' reporting, officials have not documented, as suggested by best practices, how it will determine if the measures were successful or whether changes would be needed. Second, should future changes to the measures be warranted, BJA could improve the way it documents its decisions and incorporates feedback from stakeholders, including grantees, by recording key methods and assumptions used to guide its revision efforts.

By better adhering to best practices identified by GAO and academic literature, BJA could better ensure that its future revision efforts result in successful and reliable metrics—and that the revision steps it has taken are transparent.

In the evaluations that GAO reviewed, drug-court program participation was generally associated with lower recidivism.

GAO's analysis of evaluations reporting recidivism data for 32 programs showed that drug-court program participants were generally less likely to be re-arrested than comparison group members drawn from criminal court, with differences in likelihood reported to be statistically significant for 18 of the programs.

Cost-benefit analyses showed mixed results. For example:

- Across studies showing re-arrest differences, the percentages of drug-court program participants re-arrested were lower than for comparison group members by 6 to 26 percentage points. Drug court participants who completed their program had re-arrest rates 12 to 58 percentage points below those of the comparison group.
- GAO's analysis of evaluations reporting relapse data for eight programs showed that drug-court program participants were less likely than comparison group members to use drugs, based on drug tests or self-reported drug use, although the difference was not always significant.
- Of the studies assessing drug-court costs and benefits, the net benefit ranged from positive $47,852 to negative $7,108 per participant.

December 9, 2011

The Honorable Patrick Leahy
Chairman

The Honorable Chuck Grassley
Ranking Member
Committee on the Judiciary United States Senate

The Honorable Lamar Smith
Chairman

The Honorable John Conyers, Jr.
Ranking Member
Committee on the Judiciary
House of Representatives

Drug court programs were established beginning in the late 1980s as a local response to increasing numbers of drug-related cases and expanding jail and prison populations nationwide. A drug court is a specialized court-based program that targets criminal offenders who have alcohol and other drug addiction and dependency problems.

Drug courts have implemented deferred prosecution or post-adjudication case-processing approaches, or have blended both in their organizational structures. In drug courts using deferred prosecution, defendants waive rights to a trial and enter a treatment program shortly after being charged; those who subsequently fail to complete the treatment program have their charges adjudicated, while those who complete the program are not prosecuted further, or have their charges dismissed. In post-adjudication case processing, defendants are tried and convicted, but either have deferred sentences or suspensions of incarceration until they complete or withdraw from the treatment program.

The first approach offers individuals the opportunity to obtain treatment and avoid the possibility of a felony conviction, while the second provides a rehabilitation incentive because treatment progress is factored into the sentencing determination. As of June 2010, there were over 2,500 drug courts operating throughout the United States, of which about 1,400 of these target adult offenders.[1] Drug courts are generally based on a comprehensive model involving

- offender assessment;
- judicial interaction;
- monitoring (e.g., drug testing) and supervision;
- graduated sanctions and incentives; and
- treatment services.

The Department of Justice (DOJ), through its Office of Justice Programs' (OJP) Bureau of Justice Assistance (BJA), administers the Adult Drug Court Discretionary Grant Program, which provides financial and technical assistance to states, state courts, local courts, units of local government, and Indian tribal governments to develop and implement drug treatment courts.[2] The total amount BJA has awarded in grants through the program increased from about $2 million in fiscal year 2006 to $29 million in fiscal year 2010, and the number of grants it has awarded during the same period increased 588 percent. Pursuant to the Government Performance and Results Act (GPRA), DOJ requires applicants that receive funding through the program to provide data that measure the results of their work.[3]

In April 2002, we reported that DOJ had not sufficiently managed its efforts to collect performance measurement and outcome data from federally funded drug courts.[4] We recommended that DOJ take actions to address these concerns, and DOJ agreed with our recommendations and took actions in response. Appendix I provides information on the status of these recommendations. In February 2005, we studied drug courts again and reported that in most of the 27 drug-court program evaluations we reviewed, adult drug-court programs led to *recidivism* reductions—that is, reductions in new criminal offenses—during periods of time that generally corresponded to the length of the drug court program.[5] We also reported that the evidence about the effectiveness of drug court programs in reducing participants' substance-use relapse was limited and mixed.[6]

This report responds to the Fair Sentencing Act of 2010, which directed GAO to report on drug court programs.[7] We briefed your offices on our preliminary results on July 18, 2011. This report includes our final results related to the following questions: (1) What data does DOJ collect on the performance of federally funded adult drug courts, and to what extent has it used these data in making grant related decisions? And (2) What is known about the effectiveness of adult drug courts in reducing recidivism and substance-abuse relapse rates, and what are the costs and benefits of adult drug courts? In addition, appendix I of this report provides information on the extent to which DOJ has addressed the recommendations that we made in 2002 regarding drug court programs.

To address the first question, we analyzed: the reporting guidance and requirements that BJA provided in fiscal years 2007 through 2011 to grantees applying for Adult Drug Court Discretionary Grant Program funds;[8] BJA-generated grantee performance data reports from October to December 2010; and BJA's guides for managing grants and enforcing grantee compliance that were issued in fiscal year 2011. We selected 2007 as the starting point for our review because BJA implemented its Performance Measurement Tool (PMT)—an online reporting tool that supports BJA grantees' ability to collect, identify, and report performance measurement data activities funded by the award—in fiscal year 2007. We also reviewed our prior reports and internal control standards as well as other academic literature regarding effective performance management practices.[9] Further, we interviewed cognizant BJA officials about the extent to which they use grantees' performance data when engaging in these management activities, any challenges faced with ensuring grantee compliance, ongoing efforts to revise program performance metrics, and the extent to which BJA's revisions incorporate best practices we previously identified.[10]

To address the second question, we conducted a systematic review of evaluations of drug court program effectiveness issued from February 2004 through March 2011 to identify what is known about the effect of drug court programs on the recidivism of and relapse of drug involved individuals as well as the costs and benefits of drug courts.[11] We also reviewed DOJ's National Institute of Justice (NIJ)-funded Multi-Site Adult Drug Court Evaluation (MADCE), a 5-year longitudinal process, impact, and cost evaluation of adult drug courts that was issued in June 2011, a summary of which we provide in appendix II.[12] We identified the universe of evaluations to include in our review using a three-stage process. First, we identified evaluations by searching databases and Web sites. Second, we selected evaluations of adult drug court programs in the United States that report recidivism, substance use relapse, and/or costs and benefits. Third, we screened the selected studies to determine whether each met criteria for methodological soundness based on generally accepted social science principles or cost-benefit analysis criteria. From more than 260 studies in our initial group, we assessed the findings of 44 studies that met our criteria and reported on the effectiveness of 32 drug court programs or sets of programs. See appendix III for additional details on our scope and methodology.

We conducted this performance audit from November 2010 through December 2011 in accordance with generally accepted government-auditing standards. Those standards require that we plan and perform the audit to obtain sufficient, appropriate evidence to provide a reasonable basis for our findings and conclusions based on our audit objectives. We believe that the evidence obtained provides a reasonable basis for our findings and conclusions based on our objectives.

BACKGROUND

Drug court programs are designed to address the underlying cause of an offender's behavior—alcohol, drug addiction, and dependency problems. Drug court programs share several general characteristics but vary in their specific policies and procedures because of, among other things, differences in local jurisdictions and criminal justice system practices. In general, judges preside over drug court proceedings, which are called status hearings; monitor offenders' progress with mandatory drug testing; and prescribe sanctions and incentives as appropriate in collaboration with prosecutors, defense attorneys, treatment providers, and others.

Drug court programs vary in terms of the substance-abuse treatment required. However, most programs offer a range of treatment options and generally require a minimum of 1 year of participation before an offender completes the program.

Practices for determining defendants' eligibility for drug court participation vary across drug court programs, but typically involve screening defendants for their criminal history, current case information, whether they are on probation, and their substance use, which can include the frequency and type of use, prior treatment experiences, and motivation to seek treatment. In 2005, we reported that based on literature reviewed, eligible drug-court program participants ranged from nonviolent offenders charged with drug-related offenses who had substance addictions, to relatively medium risk defendants with fairly extensive criminal histories and who had failed prior substance-abuse-treatment experiences.

Appendix IV presents additional information about the general characteristics of drug court programs. As shown in appendix V, BJA, in collaboration with the National Association of Drug Court Professionals (NADCP), identified *The Key Components*, which describes the basic elements that define drug courts and offers performance benchmarks to guide implementation.[13]

BJA administers the Adult Drug Court Discretionary Grant Program to provide financial and technical assistance to states, state courts, local courts, units of local government, and Indian tribal governments to develop and implement drug treatment courts.[14] Through the Adult Drug Court Discretionary Grant Program, BJA offers funding in four broad drug-court grant categories. See appendix VI for a more detailed discussion on each of the following grant categories.

- Implementation grants: Available to jurisdictions that have completed a substantial amount of planning and are ready to implement an adult drug court.
- Enhancement grants: Available to jurisdictions with a fully operational (at least 1-year) adult drug court.
- Statewide grants: Available for two purposes: (1) To improve, enhance, or expand drug court services statewide through activities such as training and/or technical assistance programs for drug court teams and (2) To financially support drug courts in local or regional jurisdictions that do not currently operate with BJA Adult Drug Court Discretionary Grant Program funding.
- Joint grants: In fiscal year 2010, BJA, in collaboration with the Department of Health and Human Services, Substance Abuse and Mental Health Services Administration (SAMHSA), offered a joint grant program for the enhancement of adult drug court services, coordination, and substance-abuse treatment capacity.[15]

From fiscal years 2006 through 2010, Congress appropriated about $120 million for DOJ's administration of all drug court programs.[16] Of this amount, $76 million was used for the Adult Drug Court Discretionary Grant Program, which includes funding provided to grantees through the previously mentioned grant categories.

The grant award totals for the Adult Drug Court Discretionary Grant Program increased from $2 million in fiscal year 2006 to $29 million in fiscal year 2010.[17]

Correspondingly, the number of Adult Drug Court Discretionary Grant Program awards increased from 16 in fiscal year 2006 to 110 in fiscal year 2010—an increase of 588 percent, as shown in figure 1.[18]

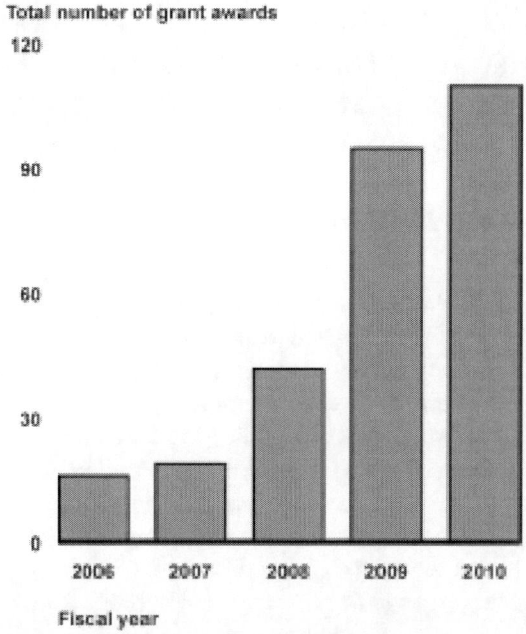

Source: GAO analysis of Bureau of Justice Assistance data.

Figure 1. Number of Adult Drug Court Discretionary Grant Program Awards Increased 588 Percent from Fiscal Year 2006 through 2010.

With regard to drug courts' effectiveness, however, drug courts have been difficult to evaluate because they are so varied, and the resources required to conduct a study that would allow conclusions about the effectiveness of drug courts can be substantial. In particular, while drug courts generally adhere to certain key program components, drug courts can differ in factors including admission criteria, type and duration of drug treatment, degree of judicial monitoring and intervention, and application of sanctions for noncompliance. In February 2005, we studied drug courts and reported that in most of the 27 drug-court program evaluations we reviewed, adult drug court programs led to recidivism reductions during periods of time that generally corresponded to the length of the drug court program.[19] Several syntheses of multiple drug court program evaluations, conducted in 2005 and 2006, also concluded that drug courts are associated with reduced recidivism rates, compared to traditional correctional options. However, the studies included in these syntheses often had methodological limitations, such as the lack of equivalent comparison groups and the lack of appropriate statistical controls.[20]

BJA IS EXPANDING USE OF GRANTEE PERFORMANCE DATA BUT COULD ENHANCE PROCESSES AS IT CONTINUES TO REFINE PERFORMANCE MEASURES

BJA's Ongoing Data Collection Efforts

> The Performance Measurement Tool (PMT) is an online reporting tool that supports BJA grantees' ability to collect, identify, and report performance-measurement data activities funded by the award. OJP's Grants Management System (GMS) is an online system designed to make the grant application process easier and more efficient for grantees. GMS allows grantees to fill out forms and submit application materials online.
>
> Source: BJA.

BJA collects an array of performance data from its adult drug court grantees through its Performance Measurement Tool (PMT) and OJP's Grants Management System (GMS). Since fiscal year 2008, BJA has required grantees to submit quantitative performance data on a quarterly basis and qualitative performance information on a semi-annual basis. The quantitative information grantees submit to BJA varies depending on the type of grant awarded. For example, information that BJA can calculate based on what Implementation grantees have been required to submit quarterly includes "the percent of drug court participants who exhibit a reduction in substance use during the reporting period," "the percent of program participants who re-offended while in the drug court program," and "the number and percent of drug court graduates."

Information that BJA can calculate based on what Enhancement grantees have been required to submit includes "the increase in units of substance-abuse treatment services" and "the percent increase in services provided to participants." In addition to the quarterly reporting of quantitative performance data, all adult drug court grantees must submit progress reports semi-annually. As part of these progress reports, grantees provide qualitative or narrative responses to seven questions. Table 1 shows the seven questions to which grantees must submit narrative responses when completing their semi-annual reports.

Table 1. List of the Seven Questions to Which Adult Drug Court Grantees Must Submit Narrative Responses

1. What were your accomplishments within this reporting period?
2. What goals were accomplished, as they relate to your grant application?
3. What problems/barriers did you encounter, if any, within the reporting period that prevented you from reaching your goals or milestones?
4. Is there any assistance that BJA can provide to address any problems/barriers identified in question number three above?
5. Are you on track to fiscally and programmatically complete your program as outlined in your grant application?
6. Based on your knowledge of the criminal justice field, are there any innovative programs/accomplishments that you would like to share with BJA?

Source: BJA.

Recent Steps to Improve Use of Performance Data

BJA officials told us that grant managers regularly review individual grantees' quarterly performance data and semi-annual progress reports and use this information to determine whether additional training or technical assistance could improve their performance.

However, according to BJA officials, resource constraints in the past had prevented staff from fully analyzing the performance data BJA collects from *all* adult drug court grantees—specifically the analysis of grantees' answers to the seven narrative questions—to identify more effective program approaches and processes to share with the drug court community. In early fiscal year 2011, BJA officials initiated a new process called GrantStat to maximize the use of performance information by leveraging the resources of other BJA divisions,[21] BJA's training and technical assistance partners, its contractor, and other key stakeholders.[22]

GrantStat provides an analytical framework to assess grantee performance data and other relevant information on a semi-annual basis to determine the effectiveness of the grant programs in BJA's portfolio.

In September 2011, BJA officials applied GrantStat to a review of the Adult Drug Court Discretionary Grant Program. As part of the process, they collected, reviewed, and analyzed performance data and other relevant information from a cohort of Implementation grantees to determine the overall effectiveness of the adult drug court program and to identify grantees that might need additional technical assistance to improve their outcomes. BJA officials told us that as part of the GrantStat review, they and their technical-assistance provider's staff reviewed selected Implementation grantees' responses to the seven narrative questions and discussed common issues they each identified.

For example, BJA identified that a number of grantees had lower-than-expected capacity because drug court stakeholders (e.g., district attorneys) were referring fewer drug-involved defendants to these drug courts. BJA also reported reviewing and discussing other qualitative information, such as the training and technical assistance provider's site-visit reports, to determine grantees' fidelity to the 10 key components.[23] BJA officials acknowledged that prior to GrantStat, they had not leveraged the summary data that its technical assistance providers had previously compiled from grantees' narrative responses to these seven questions and indicated that future iterations of GrantStat would continue to include both qualitative and quantitative performance data reviews.

Our prior work has emphasized the importance of using performance data to inform key decisions[24] and underscored that performance measures can be used to demonstrate the benefits of a program or identify ways to improve it.[25] In addition, we also have reported that effective performance measurement systems include steps to use performance information to make decisions. In doing so, program managers can improve their programs and results.26 Recognizing that BJA is working through GrantStat to improve its use of performance data in managing the drug court program, we identified six management activities for which performance information can be most useful to decision makers and benchmarked BJA's practices against them.[27] The six activities are: (1) setting program priorities, (2) allocating resources, (3) adopting new program approaches, (4) identifying and sharing with stakeholders more effective program processes and approaches, (5) setting expectations for grantees, and (6) monitoring grantee performance. See appendix VII for the definition of the six management activities. As illustrated in table 2, BJA has current and planned efforts underway across all six activities.

Table 2. Types of Information BJA Officials Reported Using or Planning to Use When Performing Key Management Activities for the Adult Drug Court Grant Program

Key management activities GAO identified	Current or prior use of performance grantee data	Planned or proposed use of grantee data
1. Setting program priorities	BJA officials reported using a range of information when setting program priorities including NIJ-sponsored research, other drug court evaluations, NADCP's annual problem-solving court census, input from state drug court coordinators, and grantee quantitative performance data to set program priorities.	BJA officials stated that they have finalized grantees' quantitative performance measures and plan to use GrantStat to identify the most effective grantees and their common characteristics. They told us that through GrantStat they plan to systematically assess performance information to prioritize which types of drug courts BJA should fund in future grant solicitations.
2. Allocating resources	BJA officials reported regularly using grantees' quantitative performance data when deciding the level of funding to be allocated toward technical assistance annually and the types of technical assistance grantees need to improve their performance.	BJA officials reported the revised quantitative performance measures will allow BJA to analyze information across all grant categories (e.g., Enhancement, Implementation, and Statewide) to determine how grantees are performing relative to one another and then allocate funding and other resources accordingly.
3. Adopting new program approaches or changing work processes	BJA officials reported that they use grantees' quantitative data to revise training courses for the program and in drafting the program's grant solicitations.	BJA officials stated the revised quantitative measures will allow them to conduct more sophisticated analyses through GrantStat. As a result, BJA officials expect to be able to identify not only the grantees that are underperforming, but also the reasons why, and then target the appropriate technical

Table 2. (Continued)

Key management activities GAO identified	Current or prior use of performance grantee data	Planned or proposed use of grantee data
		assistance to those in the most need. For example, BJA officials reported that the revised measures will help determine the extent to which grantees have adopted evidence-based practices, such as the seven design features highlighted in the MADCE study.[a]
4. Identifying and sharing with stakeholders more effective program processes and approaches	According to BJA officials, because of resource constraints, BJA had been unable to conduct analyses across all grantees' responses to the seven narrative questions in their semi-annual progress reports. As a result, the officials had not used this qualitative data when carrying out this activity. Instead, they reported using information gathered in site visits, desk reviews, and technical assistance assessments, as well as MADCE and other NIJ-sponsored research and drug court evaluations to identify effective drug court processes and procedures. BJA officials stated that information from NIJ-sponsored research and drug court evaluations is disseminated to stakeholders through the BJA-NIJ Research to Practice initiative.[b]	BJA officials stated that GrantStat will address BJA's difficulties with collectively analyzing grantee performance data on a regular basis by leveraging internal and external resources. They also stated that future GrantStat reviews will allow BJA to identify high-performing grantees and share their success stories with other grantees.
5. Setting expectations for grantees	BJA officials said that they have been unable to utilize adult drug-court program grantees' quantitative performance data to set	BJA's revised quantitative performance measures include benchmarks and other performance indicators allowing BJA to use

Key management activities GAO identified	Current or prior use of performance grantee data	Planned or proposed use of grantee data
	grantees' expectations because the measures lacked benchmarks against which to gauge grantee performance.	grantees' data to establish the targets and goals that grantees are expected to achieve. According to BJA officials, some of these performance indicators were established as part of GrantStat's first review of the program and will be communicated in the 2012 Adult Drug Court Discretionary Grant Program solicitation announcement. These indicators are based on grantee cohort averages, individual grantees' 4-year data averages, and adult drug court averages obtained from adult drug court research.
6. Monitoring grantee performance	According to BJA officials, they have analyzed individual grantees' performance data on a regular basis and provide training and technical assistance as warranted. However, according to BJA officials, because of resource constraints, BJA had been unable to conduct analyses across all grantees' responses to the seven narrative questions in their semi-annual progress reports. As a result, they had not used this qualitative information when carrying out this activity. They also acknowledged that prior to GrantStat, they had not leveraged the summary data that its technical assistance providers prepared based on	BJA officials reported the revised quantitative measures will improve BJA's ability to compare grantees' performance results with established targets and goals to determine the extent to which grantees have met them and, if necessary, to target program resources (e.g., technical assistance) to improve underperforming grantees' performance. BJA officials also told us that GrantStat's review included an assessment of the narrative responses and would continue to include it in the future.

Table 2. (Continued)

Key management activities GAO identified	Current or prior use of performance grantee data	Planned or proposed use of grantee data
	grantees' responses, despite recognizing its utility.	

Source: GAO analysis of types of information BJA officials reported using when performing management activities.

[a]The seven design features include: (1) screening and assessment, (2) target population, (3) procedural and distributive justice behavior, (4) judicial interaction, (5) monitoring, (6) treatment and other services, and (7) relapse prevention and community integration. According to DOJ officials, the seven principles were developed with NIJ on the basis of MADCE, and other rigorous research studies. The language used to describe the seven principles was determined in consultation with BJA's drug court training and technical assistance providers.

[b]The Adult Drug Court Research to Practice Initiative is a joint partnership between the National Center for State Courts and the Justice Programs Office of the School of Public Affairs at American University, with the purpose of disseminating information to drug court practitioners about current research relevant to the operations and services of adult drugs. The initiative was co-funded by BJA and NIJ.

According to BJA officials, after the GrantStat review, they identified trends and developed several potential findings and action items for program design changes. However, BJA officials added that since the action items originated from GrantStat's first review, they are not implementing them immediately. Instead, BJA plans to evaluate the action items over the next 6 months to ensure they are feasible and effective alternatives for improving grantee outcomes. We are encouraged by BJA's recent efforts to regularly analyze grantee performance data to determine whether the program is meeting its goals. We also are encouraged that BJA is using this information to better inform its grant-related management activities, such as setting program priorities, identifying and sharing effective processes and approaches, and setting expectations for grantees.

BJA Recently Revised Its Drug Court Performance Measures

During the course of our review, BJA revised its adult drug court program performance measures to improve their reliability and usefulness. BJA provided us with the revised measures on October 28, 2011.

According to BJA officials, unclear definitions of some of the previous measures confused grantees about what data elements they were expected to collect.

For example, officials told us that grantees may have been confused with how to measure "the number of participants admitted" and "the number of drug court participants."

Specifically, BJA officials added that their analysis of several years of data shows that some grantees reported the same number for these two measures, some grantees reported a higher number than were admitted, a few grantees reported a lesser number for the number of participants than the number admitted, and some grantees reported these two measures in each of these three ways over multiple reporting periods. According to BJA officials, such a wide degree of variability made these measures unreliable, and BJA was thus hindered from comparing grantee performance data across grantee cohorts.

BJA's performance measure revisions resulted in the following:

- All grantees are required to report on "participant level" measures. Examples of these measures include the demographic make-up of their drug court participant populations, the amount of service provided to their participants, and the geographic location of their drug courts;
- Enhancement, Joint, and Statewide grantees are required to report on participant level outcomes, such as graduation rates, to ensure consistency with measures BJA collects from Implementation grantees;
- Measures previously excluded from the PMT, such as retention rates and outcomes of participants once they complete the drug court program, are now included;
- BJA has established two sets of benchmarks as points of reference against which to gauge grantees' performance. The first set of benchmarks requires a comparison of grantees' performance against averages of drug court performance derived from research. The second set of benchmarks requires a comparison of grantees' performance to historical performance data reported to BJA by adult drug court grantees; and
- BJA revised the descriptions and the definitions of the measures to help ensure their clarity.

To revise the performance measures, BJA officials consulted with technical assistance providers and a drug court researcher to discuss possible improvements to the performance measures, reviewed drug court literature, and reviewed and analyzed BJA grantees' clarification and information requests to identify the most common problems adult drug court grantees historically experienced submitting performance information to BJA.[28] In addition, BJA obtained comments on the proposed measures from BJA staff and other DOJ stakeholders, as well as Enhancement, Implementation, Joint, and Statewide grantees.[29] BJA officials also invited all current grantees to participate in four teleconferences to obtain their feedback on the feasibility of collecting and reporting the new measures and their suggestions to improve the clarity of the measures' definitions and descriptions. BJA officials finalized the new measures in October 2011 and plan to closely monitor grantees' performance data submissions to ensure the reliability and usefulness of the measures and then revise as necessary after the first reporting period. BJA officials also stated that they expected to review the measures' overall reliability and validity after the first reporting period— October 1, 2011, through December 30, 2011.

BJA officials reported that the revised measures will strengthen the reliability and improve the usefulness of grantee performance data in making grant-related decisions. For example, BJA officials stated that reliable and useful data would help them to identify the most effective grantees and common characteristics these courts share to inform the types of drug courts the officials choose to fund in future grant solicitations. BJA officials also reported that as a result of the revision, they expect to be able to conduct more sophisticated analyses using GrantStat that are needed to inform grant-related decisions. For example, BJA officials told us that implementing benchmarks and participant level measures will enable the agency to compare similar drug courts (e.g., large-urban jurisdictions of similar size, demographic make-up, and geographic context) to one another and across jurisdictions, thereby improving BJA's understanding of grantees' impact on the populations they serve.

BJA Could Enhance Two Key Practices as It Continues to Review and Revise Its Adult Drug Court Performance Measures

BJA's process to revise its performance measures generally adhered to some of the key practices that we have identified as important to ensuring that measures are relevant and useful to decision-making. These key practices included obtaining stakeholder involvement[30] and ensuring that the measures have certain key attributes, such as clarity.[31] The key practices also describe the value of testing the measures to ensure that they are credible, reliable and valid[32] and documenting key steps throughout the revision process.[33] However, BJA could take actions to improve its efforts in these two areas. For instance, BJA officials told us that after the grantees' first reporting period concludes, they plan to assess the data that grantees submitted to ensure that the measures produce reliable and useful data over at least the first quarter of fiscal year 2012. They stated that if necessary, at that point they will then further revise the measures. Nevertheless, BJA officials have not documented how they will determine if the measures were successful or whether changes would be needed. In addition, BJA officials did not record key methods and assumptions used to guide their revision efforts, such as the feedback stakeholders provided and BJA's disposition of these comments. For example, BJA officials provided a document generally showing the original performance measure; whether it was removed, revised or replaced; and BJA's justification for the action, but this document did not demonstrate how BJA had incorporated the stakeholder feedback it considered when making its decisions. The document also did not include a link to a new performance measure in instances where an older one was being replaced. Further, BJA's justification did not include the rationale for the changes it made to 22 of the 51 performance measures. According to BJA officials, they did not document their decisions in this way because of the rapid nature of the revision process and limited staff resources. They also told us that maintaining such documentation and providing it to stakeholders held little value.

Our previous work has shown the importance of documentation to the successful development of effective performance measures.[34] In the past, we have reported that revising performance measures involves a number of aspects needing to be carefully planned and carried out and that by documenting the steps undertaken in developing and implementing the revised measures, agencies can be better assured their revisions result in effective performance measures.[35] In addition, academic literature on the best practices for developing effective performance measures states that agencies should develop products to document and guide their revision efforts. These products, among other things, can include plans for ensuring the quality and integrity of the data for full-scale implementation of the measures.[36] Further, S*tandards for Internal Control in the Federal Government* call for clear documentation of significant events, which can include assumptions and methods surrounding key decisions, and this documentation should be readily available for examination.37 As BJA moves forward in assessing the revised measures and implementing additional changes, if it deems necessary, BJA could better ensure that its efforts result in successful and reliable metrics and are transparent by documenting key methods used to guide revision efforts and an assessment of its measures. This would also help bolster the integrity of its decisions.

Drug Courts Were Associated with Lower Recidivism and Relapse Rates for Program Participants Than Criminal Courts

In the evaluations we reviewed, adult drug-court program participation was generally associated with lower recidivism. Our analysis of evaluations reporting recidivism data for 32 programs showed that drug court program participants were generally less likely to be re-arrested than comparison group members drawn from the criminal court system, although the differences in likelihood were reported to be statistically significant in 18 programs.[38] Across studies showing re-arrest differences, the percentages of drug court program participants rearrested were lower than for comparison group members by 6 to 26 percentage points.

One program did not show a lower re-arrest rate for all drug-court program participants relative to the comparison group within 3 years of entry into the program, although that study did show a lower re-arrest rate for drug court participants who had completed the program than for members of the comparison group.

In general, the evaluations we reviewed found larger differences in re-arrest rates between drug-court program completers and members of the comparison group than between all drug-court program participants and the comparison group members. The rearrest rates for program completers ranged from 12 to 58 percentage points below those of the comparison group.[39] The completion rates reported in the evaluations we reviewed ranged from 15 percent to 89 percent.

Included among the evaluations we reviewed was the MADCE, a 5-year longitudinal process, impact, and cost evaluation of adult drug courts. The MADCE reported a re-arrest rate for drug court participants that was 10 percentage points below that of the comparison group; specifically, 52 percent of drug court participants were re-arrested after the initiation of the drug court program, while 62 percent of the comparison group members were re-arrested.[40]

However, the 10 percentage point difference between these rearrest rates for the samples of drug court participants and comparison group members was not statistically significant.

The MADCE study also reported that drug court participants were significantly less likely than the comparison group to self-report having committed crimes when they were interviewed 18 months after the baseline (40 percent vs. 53 percent), and drug court participants who did report committing crimes committed fewer than comparison group members.

We assigned a numerical rating to each evaluation to reflect the quality of its design and the rigor of the analyses conducted. Our methodology for rating the evaluation studies is detailed in appendix III. After assigning the rating, we grouped the studies into two tiers.

Tier 1 studies were the most carefully designed and incorporated substantial statistical rigor in their analyses.

Tier 2 studies, while still meeting our basic criteria for methodological soundness, were relatively less rigorous in their design and analyses. Both tier 1 and tier 2 studies reported differences between drug court participants and comparison group members and both sets of studies found that some but not all differences were statistically significant.[41]

Table 3 shows whether a difference in recidivism rates was reported for each program—expressed as the difference in the rate of re-arrest between all drug court program participants and the comparison group. In some cases the difference in recidivism was reported as something other than a difference in the re-arrest rate, such as a difference in the number of arrests or the relative odds of an arrest.

In those cases, table 3 notes that a difference was reported, but does not include the difference in rearrest rates.

For example, the evaluation of the Queens Misdemeanor Treatment Court reported that the re-arrest rate for program participants was 14 percentage points lower than the re-arrest rate of comparison group members up to 2 years after participants entered into the program, and 10 percentage points lower at 3 or more years after entry. Similarly, the evaluation of the Hillsborough County Adult Drug Court reported a statistically significant difference in the relative odds of an arrest after drug court program enrollment but did not report the difference in rearrest rates, therefore table 3 indicates a statistically significant reduction in rearrest rates but does not show the difference in rates.

Table 3. Differences in Reported Rearrest Rates between Drug Court Program Participants and Comparison Group Members

			Percentage point difference in rate of re-arrest where reported, time frame covered		
Drug court program (state)	Reduction reported?	Reduction statistically significant?[a]	Up to 1 year after entry	Up to 2 years after entry	3 or more years after entry
Tier 1 Evaluations	Yes				
Breaking the Cycle Program (Florida)	Yes	No	-10%[b]		
Hillsborough County Adult Drug Court (Florida)	Yes[c]	Yes			
Baltimore City Drug Treatment Court (Maryland)	Yes	No			-9% -8%[d]
Queens Misdemeanor Treatment Court (New York)	Yes	Yes		-14%*	-10%*
Multnomah County Drug Court (Oregon)	Yes[e]	Yes			
MADCE (Multiple States)	Yes	No		-10%	
Breaking the Cycle Program (Washington)	Yes	Yes	-10%*[f]		
Tier 2 Evaluations	Yes				
Multiple Drug Courts (California)	Yes	Not reported			-12%
Sacramento Drug Court (California)	Yes	Not reported		-20%	
Guam Adult Drug Court (Guam)	Yes	Yes[g]			-20%
Ada County Drug Court (Idaho)	Yes	Yes			-25%*[h]
Multiple Drug Courts (Idaho)	Yes	Yes			
Monroe County Drug Treatment Court (Indiana)	Yes	Not reported		-16%	
St. Joseph County Drug Court (Indiana)	Yes	Not reported		-16%	
Vanderburgh County Day Reporting Drug Court (Indiana)	Yes	Yes[j]		-9%	
Baltimore City Circuit Court Adult Drug Treatment Court and Felony Diversion Initiative (Maryland)	Yes	Yes[j]			
Baltimore City District Court Adult Drug Treatment Court (Maryland)	Yes[k]	No			
Harford County District Court Adult Drug Court (Maryland)	Yes	Yesj			
Howard County District Court Drug Treatment Court (Maryland)	Yes	No	-13%	-10%	
Montgomery County Adult Drug Court (Maryland)	Yes	Yes	26%*	-19%*	
Prince George's County Circuit Court Adult Drug Court (Maryland)	Yes	No		0%	+1%
Wicomico County Circuit Court Adult Drug Treatment Court (Maryland)	Yes	Yes	-24%*	-18%	

			Percentage point difference in rate of re-arrest where reported, time frame covered		
Drug court program (state)	Reduction reported?	Reduction statistically significant?[a]	Up to 1 year after entry	Up to 2 years after entry	3 or more years after entry
Suffolk County Drug Court (Massachusetts)	Yes	Yes		-6%*	
Barry County Adult Drug Court (Michigan)	Yes	Not reported		-24%	
Kalamazoo County Adult Drug Treatment Court (Michigan)	Yes	Yes[j]		-14%	
Unnamed Drug Court (Midwest)	Yes[l]	No			
Kings County District Attorney's Office Drug Treatment Alternative to Prison Program (New York)	Yes	Yes	-22%	-18%*	-22%* (3 yrs) -26%* (4 yrs)
Multiple Drug Courts (Ohio)	Yes[m]	Yes		-18%	
Multnomah County Clean Court (Oregon)	Yes	Not reported	-16%		
Marion County Adult Drug Court (Oregon)	Yes	Not reported		-14%	
Multiple Drug Courts (Oregon)	Yes	Yes			-12%*
Rutland County Adult Drug Court (Vermont)	Yes	Yes			-23%*

Source: GAO analysis of drug court program evaluations.

*The difference was reported to be statistically significant.

[a] Indicates whether a reduction in any measure of recidivism reported by the study was statistically significant.

[b] Study reported a difference in recidivism of -9% for self-reported criminal acts.

[c] Study reported a statistically significant difference in the relative odds of an arrest between 12 and 18 months after drug court program enrollment.

[d] Reflects findings from 2 studies of the same drug court by the same author. See, Gottfredson et al.

[e] Study reported a 17% reduction in re-arrest rates over 5 years, but the difference in rates was not reported.

[f] Study reported a difference in recidivism of -15% for self-reported criminal acts.

[g] Study reported a statistically significant difference in the average number of arrests resulting in court filings after program initiation between the treatment and comparison groups, but did not report the significance of the difference in rates of arrest resulting in court case filings.

[h] Study reported a statistically significant difference in the rate of new court filings following program initiation. Statistical controls, if any, were not presented.

[i] Study reported a statistically significant difference in the rate of new court filings following program initiation for program completers. Statistical controls, if any, were not presented.

[j] While the differences in rearrest rates were not reported as significant, or not reported at all, study did report a statistically significant difference in average number of re-arrests between the treatment and comparison groups.

[k] Re-arrest rates for drug court participants were lower than for comparison group members for some years over a 10-year period, but none of the differences was statistically significant.

[l] Study reported a difference in re-arrest rates of -12% for program completers vs. the comparison group, which was not statistically significant.

[m] Findings reflect a comparison group that combines multiple courts.

The evaluations we reviewed showed that adult drug-court program participation was also associated with reduced drug use. Our analysis of evaluations reporting relapse data for eight programs showed that drug court program participants were less likely than comparison group members to use drugs, based on drug tests or self-reported drug use, although the difference was not always significant.[42] This was true for both within-program and post-program measures, and whether drug use was reported as the difference in the frequency of drug use or the proportion of the treatment and comparison groups who used drugs.

The MADCE concluded drug courts produce significant reductions in drug relapse. Specifically, MADCE reported that "drug court participants were significantly less likely than the comparison group to report using all drugs (56 vs. 76 percent) and also less likely to report using 'serious' drugs (41 vs. 58 percent), which omit marijuana and 'light' alcohol use (fewer than four drinks per day for women or less than five drinks per day for men). On the 18-month oral fluids drug test, significantly fewer drug court participants tested positive for illegal drugs (29 vs. 46 percent). Further, among those who tested positive or self-reported using drugs, drug court participants used drugs less frequently than the comparison group." Regarding post-drug court program relapses, the MADCE concluded that participation in drug court—along with less frequent drug use among offenders prior to arrest, and the absence of mental health problems—were the strongest predictors of success against relapses. Table 4 summarizes results of drug-use relapse reported in evaluations we reviewed.

Table 4. Drug Use Relapse Results of Evaluations GAO Reviewed

Drug court program (state)	Results of drug use relapse
Drug tests	
Barry County Adult Drug Court (Michigan)	Reduction within-program: Drug court participants generally had fewer positive drug test results than the comparison group in the 12-month period following program initiation.
St. Joseph County Drug Court (Indiana)	Reduction within-program: At all times during a 12-month period following program initiation, the drug court participants had a lower percentage of positive urine drug screens than the comparison group sample.
Vanderburgh County Day Reporting Drug Court (Indiana)	Reduction within-program: At all times during the 12-month period following program initiation, the drug court participants had a lower percentage of positive urine drug screens than the comparison group.
Methamphetamine Treatment Project (California)	Reduction within-program: Results show that drug court participants were significantly more likely than comparison participants to provide a higher proportion of clean urine samples, 97.3 percent versus 90.5 percent, respectively.
	Reduction post-program: There were substantial reductions in methamphetamine use over time for drug court participants compared to non-drug court comparison participants at program completion, and at 6 and 12 months following program completion.
Self-reported drug use	
Baltimore City Drug Treatment Court (Maryland)	Reduction post-program: Participants in the treatment group had about 27 fewer days of alcohol use, 19 fewer days of cocaine use, and 28 fewer days of heroin use on average compared to the control group. The differences were statistically significant only for the effect on cocaine. Among participants originating in the circuit court, the average number of days of cocaine use was 50 days lower in the treatment group than the control group.
Breaking the Cycle (Florida)	Reduction within-program: Approximately 9 months after the initial arrest, drug court participants were less likely to report drug use in the past 30 days (24 percent) than the comparison group (33 percent); however, this difference was not significant at the 95 percent level.
Breaking the Cycle (Washington)	Reduction within-program: Approximately 9 months after the initial arrest, there was no significant difference between the percentage of drug court participants (50 percent) and the comparison group (51percent) who self-reported drug use in the past 30 days.
Both drug tests and self-reported use	

Table 4. (Continued)

Drug court program (state)	Results of drug use relapse
MADCE (Multiple States)	Reduction 18 months after program initiation: 56 percent of drug court participants reported using any drugs compared with 76 percent among the comparison group; 41 percent of the drug court participants reported using "serious" drugs (not marijuana or light alcohol use) compared with 58 percent among the comparison group. 29 percent of drug court participants tested positive for illegal drugs compared with 46 percent of the comparison group. Among those who tested positive or self-reported using drugs, drug court participants used drugs less frequently than the comparison group.

Source: GAO analysis of adult drug court program evaluations.

Drug Court Programs Were Associated with Both Positive and Negative Net Benefits

Of the studies we reviewed, 11 included sufficient information to report a net benefit figure. Of these studies, the net benefit ranged from positive $47,852 to negative $7,108 per participant. The net benefit is the monetary benefit of reduced recidivism accrued to society from the drug court program through reduced future victimization and justice system expenditures, less the net costs of the drug court program—that is, the cost of the program less the cost of processing a case in criminal court. A negative net benefit value indicates that the costs of the drug court program outweigh its estimated benefits and that the program was not found to be cost beneficial. Eight of the studies reported positive net benefits—the benefits estimated to accrue from the drug court program exceeded the program's net costs. Three of the 11 studies reported negative net benefits. We did not attempt to determine whether the differences in the reported values were because of differences in study methodology or the attributes of the drug courts themselves. The environment in which the drug court operates may also be important. For example, the largest net benefit reported was for Kings County, in which members of the comparison group were incarcerated, in contrast to other programs in which members of the comparison group were given probation, which is less costly. The more costly the alternative, such as incarceration, the more likely a drug court will have positive net benefits. In this case, the study reported that society would accrue $47,852 in benefits relative to conventional court processing.

Table 5 below shows whether, based on the available information, the study was shown to be cost beneficial. It also shows the net benefits per participant of the drug court study. For example, MADCE found that the drug court participants led to a net benefit of $6,208 per participant— within the range of the other studies.[43] The MADCE analysis of costs and benefits is discussed further in appendix II.

Table 5. Cost Conclusions of the 11 Drug Court Program Evaluations in Our Cost-Benefit Review

Drug court program (state)	Program shown to be cost beneficial?	Net benefits
Kings County District Attorney's Office Drug Treatment Alternative to Prison Program (New York)[a]	Yes	$47,836
Multiple Drug Courts (Maine)	Yes	$42,177
Douglas County Drug Court (Nebraska)	Yes	$11,336
Multnomah County Drug Court (Oregon)	Yes	$10,826
MADCE (Multiple States)	Yes[b]	$6,208
Multiple Drug Courts (Kentucky)	Yes	$5,446
St. Joseph County Drug Court (Indiana)	Yes	$3,148
St. Louis City Adult Felony Drug Court (Missouri)	Yes	$2,615
Vanderburgh County Day Reporting Drug Court (Indiana)	No	($1,640)
Barry County Adult Drug Court (Michigan)	No	($3,552)
Monroe County Drug Treatment Court (Indiana)	No	($7,108)

Source: GAO of drug court program evaluations.

[a] Comparison was to prison population.

[b] Because of the variability in the estimate, the MADCE study could not determine that the net benefits were statistically significant. Most other studies did not report on whether differences in cost were statistically significant.

CONCLUSION

During the course of our review, BJA made strides in managing its adult drug court program, including implementation of the GrantStat process and recent revisions to the grantee performance measures. Given that BJA has committed to testing its new measures during this first grantees' reporting period, enhancements could be made to facilitate this assessment. By documenting how it plans to assess the measures and determine any changes that may be needed and providing the rationale for future revisions, BJA could bolster the transparency and integrity of its decisions. Doing so could also improve the reliability of the data it collects, its usefulness to managers in guiding the program, and the success of its measures.

RECOMMENDATION FOR EXECUTION ACTION

Recognizing that BJA has recently revised the adult drug-court performance measures and has plans to assess their utility, we recommend that BJA's Director take the following action to ensure that its revision process is transparent and results in quality and successful metrics to inform management's key decisions on program operations:

- Document key methods used to guide future revisions of its adult drug-court program performance measures. This documentation should include both a plan for how BJA will assess the measures after conclusion of the grantees' first reporting period and a rationale for why each measure was refined, including a discussion of the scope and nature of any relevant stakeholder comments.

AGENCY COMMENTS

We provided a draft of this report to DOJ for review and comment. DOJ concurred with our recommendation and described actions under way or planned to address the recommendation. DOJ also provided technical comments, which we incorporated as appropriate.

DOJ stated that BJA will continue to document grantee feedback and will ensure that revisions to the measures are documented in accordance with GAO's best practices standards. In particular, DOJ stated that BJA will document (1) whether the name and definition of the measure is consistent with the methodology used to calculate it; (2) whether the measure is reasonably free from bias; (3) whether the measure meets the expectation of the program; and (4) its rationale for why each performance measure was refined, including the scope and nature of any relevant stakeholder comments. We believe that such actions would improve the reliability of the information collected, its usefulness to managers in making key decisions on program operations, and the success of its measures.

David C. Maurer
Director, Homeland Security and Justice Issues

APPENDIX I. DOJ HAS FULLY IMPLEMENTED MOST OF OUR 2002 RECOMMENDATIONS AND PLANS TO ADDRESS THE REMAINING ONE

The following provides the current status of the seven recommendations we made in 2002—which have since been closed—on DOJ's collection of performance data.[1] Specifically, DOJ has fully implemented six of them and partially implemented one.[2] DOJ has plans to fully address the remaining recommendation related to analyzing performance and outcome data collected from grantees and reporting annually on the results. Table 6 reflects this status.

Table 6. Status of DOJ's Efforts to Address Recommendations We Made in 2002 on DOJ's Collection of Performance Data to Measure the Impact of Federally Funded Drug Court Programs

Recommendation	Actions to address recommendation	Status[a]
1. Develop and implement a management information system that is able to track and readily identify the universe of drug court programs DOJ funds.	BJA is currently using OJP's GMS to track and identify the universe of BJA funded drug court programs.[b] In 2009, BJA also developed the Enterprise Reporting Tool, an internal system, which allows BJA to query most, if not all, BJA databases, including GMS. BJA officials said this tool allows them to run reports on the universe of drug court	Fully implemented

Table 6. (Continued)

Recommendation	Actions to address recommendation	Status[a]
	programs funded by grant type, amount awarded, status, year awarded, and jurisdiction	
2. Reinstate the collection of postprogram data, selectively spot checking grantee responses to ensure accurate reporting.	On October 28, 2011, BJA provided us with the revised performance measures for the Adult Drug Court Discretionary Grant Program—which includes the data requirement for grantees to track drug-court program participants following their program completion. According to BJA officials, data collection on the revised measures will take effect with grant activities on October 1, 2011, through December 30, 2011. Data entry and reporting by grantees in the Performance Management Tool (PMT) will begin on January 1, 2012.[c] BJA officials reported concerns regarding the usefulness and reliability of postprogram data, emphasizing that once the drug court grants expire, drug courts are no longer required to track participants or report their status to BJA. BJA reported that it will test this new measure (post-program data), along with all other revised measures, and monitor for reliability in the data it receives from grantees. Having these new measures	Fully implemented

Recommendation	Actions to address recommendation	Status[a]
	in place could help ensure BJA has the program management data it needs to make informed grantee decisions.	
3. Take immediate steps to accelerate the funding and implementation of a methodologically sound national impact evaluation and consider ways to reduce the time needed to provide information on the overall impact of federally funded drug court programs.	In 2002, NIJ commissioned the adult drug court evaluation (MADCE) that selected multiple sites from across the country for review. In June 2011, MADCE was issued, and the main objectives were to: (1) test whether drug courts reduce drug use, crime, and multiple other problems associated with drug abuse, in comparison with similar offenders not exposed to drug courts; (2) address how drug courts work and for whom by isolating key individual and program factors that make drug courts more or less effective in achieving their desired outcomes; (3) explain how offender attitudes and behaviors change when they are exposed to drug courts and how these changes help explain the effectiveness of drug court programs; and (4) examine whether drug courts generate cost savings. The evaluation found that drug courts prevent crime and substance use and work equally well for most participant subgroups. See appendix II for a summary of the study.	Fully implemented

Table 6. (Continued)

Recommendation	Actions to address recommendation	Status[a]
4. Take steps to ensure and sustain an adequate grantee response rate by improving efforts to notify and remind grantees of their reporting requirements.	In fiscal year 2007, BJA began using GMS to send notifications to remind grantees of upcoming due dates for progress reports. If a progress report is more than 15 days late, GMS automatically freezes the grantee's available funding until the report is submitted. Similarly, the grantee is unable to draw down funds on a grant if a financial report is more than one day late. BJA officials said that these procedures provide an additional tool to assist grant managers in providing adequate oversight of grantees' reporting activities to ensure compliance with reporting requirements.	Fully implemented
5. Take corrective action toward grantees that do not comply with data collection reporting requirements.	In fiscal year 2007, OJP implemented a policy whereby available grant funds are frozen for noncompliant grantees that are delinquent in submitting semi-annual progress reports or quarterly financial reports. In addition, BJA has the ability to designate a grantee as high risk if the grantee continues to be noncompliant in reporting requirements. Once grantees are notified of their high-risk designation, all new awards to the grantee include high-risk special conditions that provide for additional oversight, as	Fully implemented

Recommendation	Actions to address recommendation	Status[a]
	necessary, and restrict the grantee from obligating, expending, or drawing down funds under the new awards from DOJ.	
6. Analyze performance and outcome data collected from grantees and report annually on the results.	Since 2007, using PMT, BJA has collected quarterly quantitative performance data from federally funded drug court grantees. Semi-annually, BJA also collects responses to seven narrative questions that grantees provide using PMT. BJA officials said they regularly analyze the numeric data and publish the results of the performance measure reporting on BJA's Web site. BJA does not fully analyze and report on the grantees' responses to the narrative questions. As mentioned, on October 28, 2011, BJA provided us with the revised adult drug-court program performance measures, which include measures previously excluded from PMT, such as retention rates and outcomes of participants once they complete the p rogram. As noted, BJA plans to reassess the reliability of the measures after the initial grantee reporting period concludes. After this period, BJA officials explained that they will make any necessary revisions or changes to the measures—then analyze and report on the results. As mentioned previously, BJA	Partially implemented; BJA plans to fully implement

Table 6. (Continued)

Recommendation	Actions to address recommendation	Status[a]
	initiated a new process called GrantStat to maximize the use of performance information—providing an analytical framework to assess grantee performance data and other relevant information on a semi-annual basis to determine the effectiveness of the grant programs in BJA's portfolio.	
7. Consolidate the multiple DOJ-funded drug-court-program-related data collection efforts.	BJA has been using PMT to consolidate data collection efforts since 2007. According to officials, PMT allows for grantees' online performance measurement data submission and enhanced capacity for BJA to (1) aggregate grantee data across performance measures, (2) distill performance by the type of adult drug court grant, and (3) more quickly "error check" the reliability of grantees' data submissions. BJA officials said PMT allows them to query results and assess performance outcomes, which helps them make decisions when designing future grant solicitations. According to BJA officials, using PMT to consolidate the federally funded drug court program data collection efforts enables DOJ to better manage the programs.	Fully implemented

Source: BJA.

[a] The following explains the definitions we used in assessing DOJ status in addressing the recommendations. Fully implemented—DOJ provided evidence that satisfies the entire recommendation. Partially implemented—DOJ provided evidence that satisfies about half of the recommendation. Not implemented—DOJ provided no evidence that satisfies any of the recommendation.

[b] GMS is an online system designed to make the grant application process easier and more efficient for grantees. GMS allows grantees to fill out forms and submit application materials online.

[c] PMT is an online reporting tool that supports BJA grantees' ability to collect, identify, and report performance measurement data activities funded by their award.

Appendix II. MADCE Is the Most Comprehensive Study of Drug Courts to Date, but Generalizability of Findings May Be Limited

NIJ's MADCE was conducted by the Urban Institute, Center for Court Innovation, and Research Triangle Institute.[1] Data were collected from 1156 drug court participants in 23 different drug courts in 7 geographic clusters and from a comparison group of 625 drug-involved offenders in six different sites in four geographic clusters. Data collected included: three waves of interviews; drug tests; administrative records on treatment, arrests, and incarceration; court observation and interviews with staff and other stakeholders; and budget and other cost information. The evaluation was designed to address the following four questions:

1) Do drug courts reduce drug use, criminal behavior, and other associated offender problems?
2) Do drug courts generate cost savings for the criminal justice system and other public institutions?
3) Are drug courts especially effective or less effective for certain categories of offenders or program characteristics?
4) Which drug court policies and offender perceptions explain their overall impact?

MADCE FOUND REDUCTIONS IN RECIDIVISM AND RELAPSE, BUT GENERALIZABILITY MAY BE LIMITED

The MADCE's major findings can be summarized as follows:

- Drug courts produce statistically significant reductions in self-reported crime. While both the drug court participants and comparison group participants reported large numbers of crimes in the year preceding the 18-month follow-up, drug court participants reported statistically significantly fewer than the comparison group members. Drug court participants were less likely than members of the comparison group to report committing any crimes (40 percent vs. 53 percent) and drug court participants reported committing fewer crimes in the preceding 12 months than comparison group members (43 criminal acts vs. 88 criminal acts). The difference between the two groups in the probability of an official re-arrest over 24 months was not statistically significant, though the percentage of individuals rearrested was lower for the drug court group than the comparison group (52 percent vs. 62 percent), as was the average number of re-arrests (1.24 vs. 1.64).2
- Drug courts produce statistically significant reductions in drug use. Drug court participants were less likely than members of the comparison group to report using any drugs (56 percent vs. 76 percent) and any serious drugs (41 percent vs. 58 percent), and less likely to test positively for drugs at the 18-month follow-up (29 percent vs. 46 percent). Furthermore, the large difference in self-reported relapse rates is evident at 6 months (40 percent vs. 59 percent), so the impact of drug courts on alcohol and other drug use is sustained. The interview data also indicate that among the drug court participants and comparison group members that were using drugs, the drug court participants, on average, were using them less frequently.
- Drug court participants reported some benefits, relative to comparison group members, in other areas of their lives. At 18 months, drug court participants were statistically significantly less likely than comparison group members to report a need for employment, educational, and financial services, and reported statistically significantly less family conflict.

However, there were modest, non-significant differences in employment rates, income, and family emotional support, and no differences found in experiencing homelessness or depression.

- Regardless of background, most offenders who participated in drug courts had better outcomes than offenders who were in the comparison programs. However, the impact of drug courts was greater for participants with more serious prior drug use and criminal histories, and the impact was smaller for participants who were younger, male, African-American, or who had mental health problems.
- While the treatment and service costs were higher for drug court participants than treatment and service costs associated with the alternative "business-as-usual" comparison programs, drug courts save money through improved outcomes, according to the researchers, primarily through savings to victims resulting from fewer crimes and savings resulting from fewer re-arrests and incarcerations.
- The authors of the study assert that their findings have strong internal validity—that is, that the findings were actually produced by the drug court programs—and external validity—that is, that the findings can be generalized to the population of all drug court participants and potential comparison group members. The claim to strong internal validity is not without merit, given the high response rates, low attrition, propensity score adjustments, and conservative estimates produced by the hierarchical models used.3 The claim of high internal validity is also supported by the sensitivity analyses undertaken for several outcomes using other models and methods of adjustments that produced little or no change in conclusions. The claim to strong external validity, which relates to the generalizability of the results beyond the sample of courts and comparison sites and specific offenders considered, may be somewhat overstated. The authors note that the 23 drug courts included in the study represent "a broad mix of urban, suburban, and rural courts from 7 geographic clusters nationwide," but that doesn't assure that, collectively, the drug courts that were included resemble the hundreds of drug courts that were not included, especially since they were not chosen at random. It also seems unlikely that the six comparison sites from four states are representative of all potential controls, or all alternative programs in all states, and it is potentially problematic that all of the selected sites, including drug court and comparison sites, were alike in their

willingness and interest in participating. Those concerns notwithstanding, this is the broadest and most ambitious study of drug courts to date; it is well done analytically; and the results, as they relate to the impact of drug courts, are transparent and well described.

MADCE's Cost Benefit Analysis Focused on Individuals

The MADCE cost benefit analysis approach differed from most of the other studies we reviewed. In most of the other studies, the average cost and benefit of a drug court participant was compared to the average cost and benefit of normal court processing. In contrast, the MADCE obtained a separate net benefit figure for each individual. The net benefit was obtained by tracking each individual's use of resources, such as hearings or meetings with case managers, and program outcomes like use of public assistance. The MADCE also tracked each individual's rates of rearrest, number of crimes, and time of incarceration. The crimes are multiplied by cost to victims per crime to obtain the cost to society. The difference between the net benefits of the drug court participants and the comparison group were obtained using a hierarchical model similar to the one used for program outcomes. After applying the method, the MADCE found that the drug court participants led to a net benefit of $6,208[4] to society per participant, as compared to the comparison group. However, due to the variability in the estimate, the study did not find that the net benefits were statistically significant.

The lack of a statistically significant difference may be because of greater variability in the MADCE approach than the approach used in other studies. Specifically, the MADCE did not assume identical costs for each participant. As a result, costs may be higher for individuals who have lower rates of re-arrest, perhaps because those individuals received more treatment. According to the study's authors, by assuming identical costs for each participant, the standard approach understates the variance in the computed net benefit figure by not including the variability in cost. However, the MADCE authors assumed that the prices of services were consistent across sites by using a weighted average. In contrast, some studies generate site-specific cost figures. In this way, the MADCE approach did exclude one source of variation that is present in some other studies.

In addition to tracking costs and benefits at the individual level, the MADCE also included some effects of drug court participation that some other studies omit. This is consistent with OMB guidance that states that studies should be comprehensive in the benefits and costs to society considered.[5] One of the benefits considered by the MADCE, sometimes omitted elsewhere, is the estimated earnings of the drug court participant. However, it is unclear that the full value of earnings should have been considered a net benefit to society. For example, to be comprehensive, a study should also consider the cost to society of providing that benefit. The net benefit would account for the value of production from this employment less the wages paid. Although in this case, it is unlikely that this would affect the result of the analysis, as the earnings are similar for drug court participants and the comparison group.

APPENDIX III. OBJECTIVES, SCOPE AND METHODOLOGY

To determine what data DOJ collects on the performance of federally funded adult drug courts and to what extent DOJ has used this data in making grant-related decisions, we analyzed the reporting guidance and requirements that BJA provided in fiscal years 2007 through 2011 to grantees applying for Adult Drug Court Discretionary Grant Program funds;[1] BJA-generated grantee performance data reports from October to December 2010; and BJA's guides for managing grants and enforcing grantee compliance that were issued in fiscal year 2011. We selected 2007 as the starting point for our review because BJA implemented its Performance Measurement Tool (PMT)—an online reporting tool that supports BJA grantees' ability to collect, identify, and report performance-measurement data activities funded by the grantees' awards—in fiscal year 2007. We also reviewed our prior reports and internal control standards as well as other academic literature regarding effective performance-management practices.[2] We then used this information and BJA officials' statements to identify and define six management activities for which performance information can be most useful in making grant-related decisions.[3] Further, we interviewed cognizant BJA officials about the extent to which they use grantees' performance data when engaging in these management activities, any challenges faced with ensuring grantee compliance, ongoing efforts to revise program performance metrics, and the extent to which BJA's revisions incorporate best practices we previously identified.[4]

To determine what is known about the effectiveness of adult drug courts in reducing recidivism and substance-abuse relapse rates and what the costs and benefits of adult drug courts are, we conducted a systematic review of evaluations of drug-court program effectiveness issued from February 2004 through March 2011 to identify what is known about the effect of drug court programs on the recidivism of and relapse of drug-involved individuals as well as the costs and benefits of drug courts.[5] We also reviewed DOJ's NIJ-funded MADCE, a 5-year longitudinal process, impact, and cost evaluation of adult drug courts that was issued in June 2011. We identified the universe of evaluations to include in our review using a three-stage process. First, we (1) conducted key-word searches of criminal justice and social science research databases;[6] (2) searched drug court program-related Web sites, such as those of BJA and NADCP; (3) reviewed bibliographies, meta-analyses of drug court evaluations, and our prior reports on drug court programs;[7] and (4) asked drug court researchers and DOJ officials to identify evaluations. Our literature search identified 260 documents, which consisted of published and unpublished outcome evaluations, process evaluations, commentary about drug court programs, and summaries of multiple program evaluations.[8] Second, we reviewed the 260 documents our search yielded and identified 44 evaluations that reported recidivism or substance use relapse rates using either an experimental or quasi-experimental design, or analyzed program costs and benefits.[9] Third, we used generally accepted social science and cost benefit criteria to review the 44 evaluations.

To assess the methodological quality of evaluations that reported on recidivism or relapse rates, we placed each evaluation into one of five categories, with category 1 evaluations being the most rigorous and category 5 the least, as outlined in table 7.

We excluded studies that were placed in category 5 in the table above or studies in which the comparison group was not drawn from a criminal court. We were left with 33 studies, plus the MADCE, that reported on the effectiveness of 32 drug court programs or sets of programs.10 As noted in our report, we then grouped the 34 studies, including the MADCE, into two tiers according to their quality category, Tier 1 studies were those that fell into categories 1 or 2, Tier 2 studies were those that fell into categories 3 or 4.

Observed differences in recidivism could arise from measured and unmeasured sources of variation between drug court participants and comparison group members. If comparison group members differed systematically from drug court participants on variables that are also associated with recidivism, such as the degree of their substance-abuse addiction problem and these variables were not accounted for by the design or analysis used in the evaluation, then the study could suffer from selection bias wherein observed differences in recidivism could be because of these sources of variation rather than participation in the drug court program. As indicated in table 7, our evaluation of the methods used to deal with selection bias was reflected in the quality categorization of each study.[11]

Table 7. Methodological Quality Categories for Evaluations of a Drug Court Program

Category	Required methodological elements
1.	Random assignment to drug court or control group, drawn from local offenders eligible for the program. The sample: (a) is of sufficient size to ensure that randomization balances all covariates (e.g., potential predictors of outcomes, such as past criminal history); or (b) has constrained key covariates to balance in small samples through stratification (e.g., sampling subpopulations independently to improve representativeness) or through other adjustments. Randomization occurs after eligible offense, not after screening or other self-selection. Drug court is compulsory if assigned, and rates of attrition from the program are low.
2.	*Either* Random assignment with several factors in group 1 missing, such as small sample sizes or some amount of pre-screening of eligible participants; *or* Nonrandom assignment, but analysis models or controls for the specific process used to assign participants to the drug court when constructing a longitudinal comparison group. Alternatively, assignment to the program was nonrandom but clearly exogenous to the outcomes. The comparison group is similar to the treatment group on any variables the program explicitly uses to screen participants, such as "readiness for treatment" or "likely response to treatment." Comparison group is matched on multiple years of pre-treatment data.
3.	*Either* Problematic random assignment: extremely small sample sizes, many large differences between treatment and control groups, randomization that occurs after all important forms of self-selection or screening; *or* Nonrandom assignment, and the analysis controls for pre-treatment outcomes and participant demographics without considering the specific process used to assign participants to the program being evaluated. Comparison group is used, but has limited pre-treatment covariate data for construction. Comparison or treatment groups are constructed in ways that could have a clear impact on the outcomes (e.g., truncating the sample).
4.	Nonrandom assignment. Comparison group constructed with few controls for pre-treatment outcomes or shows covariate differences with the treatment group. Several plausible sources of selection bias, such as preexisting differences between the two groups in the degree of substance use.
5.	Nonrandom assignment. Cross-sectional design with few controls, pre-post design with no comparison group and few controls, or treatment group that includes only program graduates.

Source: GAO.

To assess the methodological quality of evaluations that reported on drug court program costs and benefits, we assessed them according to the five criteria we developed and outlined in table 8 below.[12]

Table 8. Five Criteria for Assessing a Cost-Benefit Analysis of a Drug Court Program

Criterion	Description
1. States the program's purpose	In general, the purpose of a drug court program is to reduce repeated criminal behavior—to reduce recidivism—by reducing offenders' substance-using behavior.
2. Identifies the baseline	The baseline, or alternative, is what would happen to an offender if the drug court program did not exist.
3. Assesses all relevant costs	The costs involved in a drug court program are those associated with the program's operation and those associated with the baseline.
4. Assesses all relevant benefits	Benefits usually attributed to drug court programs are costs avoided because of reduced recidivism; they accrue to the criminal justice system and potential victims of crime. Other benefits an analysis could consider include reduced medical costs and successful program participants' increased productivity.
5. Assesses uncertainty in cost and benefit estimates	Most cost and benefit estimates entail uncertainty from imprecision in the data underlying the analysis and the assumptions built into the analysis. Assessing uncertainty enhances confidence in the estimates used in evaluation.

Source: GAO-05-219.

We determined that an essential criterion for reporting a net benefit of drug courts was that the costs of the drug court were assessed against a baseline (i.e., "business-as-usual" or traditional court processing). Eleven studies met this essential standard and were used to report on program costs and benefits. We excluded other studies not meeting this standard even though they may have met others.

To obtain information on our outcomes of interest—that is, recidivism, substance use relapse, and costs and benefits—we used data collection instruments to systematically collect information about the methodological characteristics of each evaluation, the drug court participants and comparison group members studied, and the outcomes of the participants and other comparable groups reported. Each evaluation was read and coded by a senior social scientist, statistician, or economist with training and experience in evaluation research methods. A second senior social scientist, statistician, or economist then reviewed each completed data collection instrument to verify the accuracy of the information included. Part of our assessment also focused on the quality of the data used in the evaluations as reported by the researchers and our observations of any problems with missing data, any limitations of data sources for the purposes for which they were used, and inconsistencies in reporting data. We incorporated any data problems that we noted in our quality assessments.

We selected the evaluations in our review based on their methodological strength; therefore, our results cannot be generalized to all drug court programs or their evaluations. Although the findings of the evaluations we reviewed are not representative of the findings of all evaluations of drug court programs, the evaluations consist of those evaluations we could identify that used the strongest designs to assess drug-court program effectiveness.

To identify the extent to which DOJ has addressed the recommendations that we made in 2002 regarding drug court programs, we interviewed cognizant DOJ officials and obtained and reviewed documentation (e.g., drug-court program grant solicitations and grantee-performance reporting guidance) on the actions taken to address and implement each of our prior recommendations. We conducted this performance audit from November 2010 through December 2011 in accordance with generally accepted government-auditing standards. Those standards require that we plan and perform the audit to obtain sufficient, appropriate evidence to provide a reasonable basis for our findings and conclusions based on our audit objectives. We believe that the evidence obtained provides a reasonable basis for our findings and conclusions based on our objectives.

APPENDIX IV. OVERVIEW OF DRUG COURT PROGRAM CHARACTERISTICS

This appendix provides a general description of drug court program components (see table 9). Drug court programs rely on a combination of judicial supervision and substance-abuse treatment to motivate defendants' recovery.[1] Judges preside over drug court proceedings, which are called status hearings; monitor defendants' progress with mandatory drug testing; and prescribe sanctions and incentives, as appropriate in collaboration with prosecutors, defense attorneys, treatment providers, and others. Drug court programs can vary in terms of the substance-abuse treatment required. However, most programs offer a range of treatment options and generally require a minimum of about 1 year of participation before a defendant completes the program.

Table 9. General Description of Drug Court Program Components

Drug court elements	Description
Drug court program approaches	Drug court programs generally have taken two approaches to processing cases: (1) deferred prosecution (diversion); and (2) post-adjudication. In the diversion model, the courts defer prosecution dependent on the defendant's agreement to participate in the drug court program. Deferred adjudication models do not require the defendant to plead guilty. Instead the defendant enters the drug court before pleading to a charge. Defendants who complete the treatment program are not prosecuted further and their charges are dismissed. Failure to complete the program results in prosecution for the original offense. This approach is intended to capitalize on the trauma of arrest and offers defendants the opportunity to obtain treatment and avoid the possibility of a felony conviction. In contrast, defendants participating in a postadjudication (post-plea) drug court program plead guilty to the charge(s) and their sentences are suspended or deferred. Upon successful completion of the program, sentences are waived and in many cases records are expunged. This approach provides an incentive for the defendant to rehabilitate because progress toward rehabilitation is factored into the sentencing determination. Both of these approaches provide the defendant with a powerful incentive to complete the requirements of the drug court program. Some drug court programs use both deferred prosecution and post-adjudication approaches and assign defendants to an approach depending on the severity of the charge. Additionally, drug court programs may also combine aspects of these models into a hybrid or combined approach.
Screening process and participant eligibility criteria	Defendants reach the drug court program from different sources and at varying points in case processing. Screening defendants to determine eligibility for a drug court program generally includes assessing their criminal history and current case information (e.g., charging offense, prior convictions, pending cases, and probation status). Depending on the program, an assistant district or prosecuting attorney, court clerk, or drug court coordinator typically conducts the

Drug court elements	Description
	review. Drug courts generally accept defendants charged with drug possession or other nonviolent offenses such as property crimes. Some drug court programs allow defendants who have prior convictions to participate, and others do not. Federal grants administered by BJA may not be awarded to any drug court program that allows either current or past violent offenders to participate in its program.[a] After defendants are determined to be legally eligible for the program, treatment providers or case managers will typically determine defendants' clinical eligibility. This can be determined through structured assessment tests, interviews, or even preliminary drug test results. While drug courts generally only accept defendants with substance-abuse problems, they vary in the level of addiction or type of drug to which defendants are addicted. For example, some programs do not accept defendants who only have addictions to marijuana or alcohol, while others do. Clinical eligibility can also include factors such as medical or mental health barriers and motivation or treatment readiness. In several drug court programs in our review, the drug court judge's satisfaction with or assessment of an offender's motivation and ability to complete the program was a factor used to screen defendants.
Program completion requirements	Drug court programs typically require defendants to complete a 1-year treatment program in order to graduate from or complete the program. Some programs impose other conditions that participants must meet in addition to treatment. These conditions could include remaining drug-free for a minimum amount of time, not being arrested for a specified period of time, maintaining employment or obtaining an educational degree or certification, or performing community service.
Judicial supervision and status hearings	The central element of all drug court programs is attendance at the regularly scheduled status hearings, at which the drug court judge monitors the progress of participants. Monitoring is based on treatment-provider reports on such matters as drug testing and attendance at counseling sessions. The judge is to reinforce progress and address noncompliance with program requirements. The primary objectives of the status hearing are to keep the defendant in treatment and to provide continuing court supervision. More broadly, judicial supervision includes regular court appearances and direct in-court interaction with the judge, as well as scheduled case manager visits.
Drug-testing requirements	Monitoring participants' substance use through mandatory and frequent testing is a core component of drug court programs. Programs vary in the specific policies and procedures regarding the nature and frequency of testing. For example, in some programs in

Drug court elements	Description
	our review participants were required to call to find out whether they are required to be tested in a given period or on a randomly selected day of the week. The frequency of testing generally varied depending on the stage or phase of the program that participants were in.
Treatment components	In most drug court programs, treatment is designed to last at least 1 year and is generally administered on an outpatient basis with limited inpatient treatment, as needed, to address special detoxification or relapse situations. Many of the programs operate with the philosophy that because drug addiction is a disease, relapses can occur and that the court must respond with progressive sanctions or enhanced treatment, rather than immediate termination. Treatment services are generally divided into three phases. Detoxification, stabilization, counseling, drug education, and therapy are commonly provided during phases I and II, and in some instances, throughout the program. Other services relating to personal and educational development, job skills, and employment services are provided during phases II and III, after participants have responded to initial detoxification and stabilization. Housing, family, and medical services are frequently available throughout the program. In some instances, a fourth phase consisting primarily of aftercare-related services is provided. The objectives of drugcourt program treatment are generally to (1) eliminate the program participants' physical dependence on drugs through detoxification; (2) treat the defendant's craving for drugs through stabilization (referred to as rehabilitation stage) during which frequent group or individual counseling sessions are generally employed; and (3) focus on helping the defendant obtain education or job training, find a job, and remain drug free. Drug court programs can also either directly provide or refer participants to a variety of other services and support, and they may include medical or health care, mentoring, and educational or vocational programs. The use of community-based treatment self-help groups, such as Alcoholics Anonymous and Narcotics Anonymous, and aftercare programs also varies across drug court programs.
Sanctions for noncompliance	Judges generally prescribe sanctions and incentives as appropriate in collaboration with prosecutors, defense attorneys, treatment providers, and others. Typical sanctions for program noncompliance include oral warnings from the judge; transfer to an earlier stage of the program; attendance at more frequent status hearings, treatment sessions, or drug tests; and serving jail time for several days or weeks. The approach or philosophy for how a drug court judge prescribes sanctions can vary. For example, some judges use a graduated sanctions approach, where sanctions are applied in increasing severity. participants' noncompliance on a case-by-case basis.

Drug court elements	Description
Termination criteria	Drug court programs typically use various criteria for ending a defendant's participation in the program before completion. These criteria may include a new felony offense, multiple failures to comply with program requirements such as not attending status hearings or treatment sessions, and a pattern of positive drug tests. Before terminating a defendant for continuing to use drugs, drug court programs generally will use an array of treatment services and available sanctions. There are no uniform standards among all programs on the number of failed drug tests and failures to attend treatment sessions that lead to a participant's termination. Drug court program judges generally make decisions to terminate a program participant on a case-by-case basis, taking into account the recommendations of others, including the treatment provider, prosecutor, and defense counsel. Relapses are expected, and the extent to which noncompliance results in terminations varies from program to program. Once a defendant is terminated, he or she is usually referred for adjudication or sentencing.

Source: GAO-05-219.

[a] 42 U.S.C. § 3797u-1- u-2. Violent offenders generally include those who have been charged with or convicted of an offense that is punishable by a term of imprisonment of greater than one year, and the offense involved a firearm or dangerous weapon; death or serious bodily injury; or the use of force. Past violent offenders include those who have one or more prior convictions for a felony crime of violence involving the use or attempted use of force against a person with the intent to cause death or serious bodily harm. § 3797u-2.

APPENDIX V. TEN KEY COMPONENTS OF A DRUG COURT— DEVELOPED BY BJA IN COLLABORATION WITH THE NATIONAL ASSOCIATION OF DRUG COURT PROFESSIONALS

Table 10. Ten Key Components of a Drug Court

1. Integration of substance-abuse treatment with justice system case processing.
2. Use of a non-adversarial approach, in which prosecution and defense promote public safety while protecting the right of the participant to due process.
3. Early identification and prompt placement of eligible participants.
4. Access to continuum of treatment, rehabilitation, and related services.
5. Frequent testing for alcohol and illicit drugs.

Table 10. (Continued)

6. A coordinated strategy governs drug court responses to participants' compliance.
7. Ongoing judicial interaction with each participant.
8. Monitoring and evaluation to measure achievement of program goals and gauge effectiveness.
9. Continuing interdisciplinary education to promote effective planning, implementation, and operation.
10. Forging partnerships among drug courts, public agencies, and community-based organizations generates local support and enhances drug court program effectiveness.

Source: BJA.

APPENDIX VI. BJA OFFERS SOLICITATIONS IN FOUR BROAD DRUG-COURT GRANT CATEGORIES—IMPLEMENTATION, ENHANCEMENT, STATEWIDE, AND JOINT

As mentioned, the Adult Drug Court Discretionary Grant Program provides financial and technical assistance to states, state courts, local courts, units of local government, and Indian tribal governments to develop and implement drug treatment courts. There are four different types of awards that BJA makes to adult drug-court grantees through the program. Table 11 provides a description of the grant types.

Table 11. Adult Drug-Court Discretionary Grant Program—Grant Type and Description

Grant type	Description
Implementation grants	Available to jurisdictions that have completed planning and are ready to implement an adult drug court. Grantees may use their awards to fund various court operations and services including offender supervision, management, and services; provision and coordination of non-treatment recovery support services; and childcare and other family supportive services.
Enhancement grants	Available to jurisdictions with fully operational adult drug courts. Applicants may use funding to expand their target population, enhance court services, or enhance offender services.

Grant type	Description
Statewide grants	Used to improve, enhance, or expand drug court services statewide by encouraging adherence to the evidence-based design features and through activities such as: training and/or technical assistance programs for drug court teams geared to improve drug court functioning and to increase drug court participation and participant outcomes; tracking, compiling, coordinating, and disseminating state drug court information and resources; increasing communication, coordination, and information sharing among drug court programs; conducting a statewide drug court evaluation; or establishing a statewide automated drug-court data collection and/or performance management system.
Joint grants	BJA, in collaboration with the Department of Health and Human Services, Substance Abuse and Mental Health Services Administration (SAMHSA), offers a joint grant program for the enhancement of adult drug court services, coordination, and substance-abuse treatment capacity.[a] Successful applicants are awarded two grants: an Enhancement grant from BJA and a Behavioral Health Court Collaboration Grant from SAMHSA. This joint program offers grantees the opportunity to design a comprehensive strategy for enhancing drug court capacity while accessing both criminal justice and substance-abuse treatment funds under single grant application.

Source: BJA.

[a] SAMHSA is authorized under section 509 of the Public Health Service Act, as amended (42 U.S.C. § 290bb-2) to provide Adult Treatment Drug Court grants.

Appendix VII. Key Management Activities Identified for Which Performance Information Can Be Most Useful

Table 12. Definitions: Key Management Activities Identified for Which Performance Information Can Be Most Useful

Key management activities	How performance information may be used to support the activity
a. Setting program priorities	Performance information is used to set priorities in budgeting and to target resources. Agencies can also use this information to identify priorities on which to focus their efforts. For example, targeting grants to address "underserved" client groups.

Table 12. (Continued)

Key management activities	How performance information may be used to support the activity
b. Allocating resources	Performance information is used to compare results of agencies' programs with goals and to identify where program resources should be targeted to improve performance and achieve goals. When faced with reduced resources, such analyses can assist agencies' efforts to minimize the impact on program results.
c. Adopting new program approaches or changing work processes	Performance information is used to assess the way a program is conducted and the extent to which a program's practices and policies have or have not led to improvements in outcomes. Such information is used to identify problems and consider alternative approaches and processes in areas where goals are not being met and to enhance the use of program approaches and processes that are working well.
d. Identifying and sharing with stakeholders more effective processes and approaches to program implementation	Performance information is used to identify and increase the use of program approaches that are working well and share these effective processes and approaches with stakeholders.
e. Setting expectations for grantees	Performance information is used to establish the targets and goals that grantees are expected to achieve. These targets and goals can be used as the basis for corrective action (e.g., technical assistance, freezing of funds) or to reward high performing grantees.
f. Monitoring grantee performance	Performance information is used to compare grantees' performance results with established targets and goals to determine the extent to which grantees have met them and, if necessary, target program resources (e.g., technical assistance) to improve grantees' performance.

Source: GAO analyses.

Note: We identified the first four management activities above as relevant from governmentwide surveys of federal managers conducted in 1997, 2000, and 2003. See GAO-05-927. The remaining two activities we identified by reviewing performance management literature. In defining the management activities, we reviewed the literature identified and met with BJA officials to determine the extent to which they agreed with our definitions. BJA staff confirmed each of these six to be relevant to managing the drug court program.

REFERENCES

Bouffard, Jeffrey A., and Katie A. Richardson. "The Effectiveness of Drug Court Programming for Specific Kinds of Offenders: Methamphetamine and DWI Offenders Versus Other Drug-Involved Offenders." *Criminal Justice Policy Review*, 18(3) (September 2007): 274-293.

Carey, Shannon M., and Michael W. Finigan. *Indiana Drug Courts: St. Joseph County Drug Court Program Process, Outcome and Cost Evaluation-Final Report*. Portland, OR: NPC Research, 2007.

Carey, Shannon M., and Michael W. Finigan. *Indiana Drug Courts: Vanderburgh County Day Reporting Drug Court Process, Outcome and Cost Evaluation-Final Report*. Portland, OR: NPC Research, 2007.

Carey, Shannon M., and Michael W. Finigan. "A Detailed Cost Analysis in a Mature Drug Court Setting: A Cost-Benefit Evaluation of the Multnomah County Drug Court." *Journal of Contemporary Criminal Justice*, 20(3) (August 2004): 315-338.

Carey, Shannon M., Michael W. Finigan, et. al. *Indiana Drug Courts: Monroe County Drug Treatment Court Process, Outcome and Cost Evaluation-Final Report*. Portland, OR: NPC Research, 2007.

Carey, Shannon M., Michael Finigan, Dave Crumpton, and Mark S. Waller. "California Drug Courts: Outcomes, Costs and Promising Practices: An Overview of Phase II in a Statewide Study." *Journal of Psychoactive Drugs* (November 2006).

Carey, Shannon M., Lisa M. Lucas, Mark S. Waller, Callie H. Lambarth, Robert Linhares, Judy M. Weller, and Michael W. Finigan. *Vermont Drug Courts: Rutland County Adult Drug Court Process, Outcome, and Cost Evaluation-Final Report*. Portland, OR: NPC Research, 2009.

Carey, Shannon, and Gwen Marchand. *Marion County Adult Drug Court Outcome Evaluation-Final Report*. Portland, OR: NPC Research, 2005.

Carey, Shannon M. and Mark S. Waller. *Oregon Drug Court Cost Study: Statewide Costs and Promising Practices-Final Report*. Portland, OR: NPC Research, 2010.

Carey, Shannon M., and Mark Waller. *California Drug Courts: Costs and Benefits-Phase III*. Portland, OR: NPC Research, 2008.

Carey, Shannon M., and Mark S. Waller. *Guam Adult Drug Court Outcome Evaluation-Final Report*. Portland, OR: NPC Research, 2007.

Dandan, Doria Nour. *Sex, Drug Courts, and Recidivism*. University of Nevada, Las Vegas: 2010.

Ferguson, Andrew, Birch McCole, and Jody Raio. *A Process and Site-Specific Outcome Evaluation of Maine's Adult Drug Treatment Court Programs*. Augusta, ME: University of Southern Maine, 2006.

Finigan, Michael W., Shannon M. Carey, and Anton Cox. *Impact of a Mature Drug Court Over 10 Years of Operation: Recidivism and Costs (Final Report).* Portland, OR: NPC Research, 2007.

Gottfredson, Denice C., Brook W. Kearley, Stacy S. Najaka, and Carlos M. Rocha. "How Drug Treatment Courts Work: An Analysis of Mediators." *Journal of Research in Crime and Delinquency*, 44(1) (February 2007): 3-35.

Gottfredson, Denice C., Brook W. Kearley, Stacy S. Najaka, and Carlos M. Rocha. "Long-term effects of participation in the Baltimore City drug treatment court: Results from an experimental study." *Journal of Experimental Criminology*, 2(1) (January 2006): 67-98.

Gottfredson, Denice C., Brook W. Kearley, Stacy S. Najaka, and Carlos M. Rocha. "The Baltimore City Drug Treatment Court: 3-Year Self-Report Outcome Study." *Evaluation Review*, 29(1) (February 2005): 42-64.

Krebs, C.P., C.H. Lindquist, W. Koetse, and P.K. Lattimore. "Assessing the long-term impact of drug court participation on recidivism with generalized estimating equations." *Drug and Alcohol Dependence*, 91(1) (November 2007): 57-68.

Labriola, Melissa M. *The Drug Court Model and Chronic Misdemeanants: Impact Evaluation of the Queens Misdemeanor Treatment Court*. New York, NY: Center for Court Innovation, 2009.

Latimer, Jeff, Kelly Morton-Bourgon, and Jo-Anne Chrétien. *A Meta-Analytic Examination of Drug Treatment Courts: Do They Reduce Recidivism?* Ottawa, Ontario: Department of Justice Canada, 2006.

Listwan, Shelley Johnson, James Borowiak, and Edward J. Latessa. *An Examination of Idaho's Felony Drug Courts: Findings and Recommendations-Final Report*. Kent State University and University of Cincinnati: 2008.

Logan, T. K., William H. Hoyt, Kathryn E. McCollister, Michael T. French, Carl Leukefeld, and Lisa Minton. "Economic evaluation of drug court: methodology, results, and policy Implications." *Evaluation and Program Planning*, 27 (2004):381–396.

Loman, Anthony L. *A Cost-Benefit Analysis of the St. Louis City Adult Felony Drug Court*. Institute of Applied Research. St. Louis, MO: 2004.

Lowenkamp, Christopher T., Alexander M. Holsinger, Edward J. Latessa. "Are Drug Courts Effective: A Meta-Analytic Review." *Journal of Community Corrections*. (Fall 2005): 5-28.

Mackin, Juliette R., Shannon M. Carey, and Michael W. Finigan. *Harford County District Court Adult Drug Court: Outcome and Cost Evaluation*. Portland, OR: NPC Research, 2008.

Mackin, Juliette R., Shannon M. Carey, and Michael W. Finigan. *Prince George's County Circuit Court Adult Drug Court: Outcome and Cost Evaluation*. Portland, OR: NPC Research, 2008.

Mackin, Juliette R., Lisa M. Lucas, Callie H. Lambarth, Mark S. Waller, Shannon M. Carey, and Michael W. Finigan. *Baltimore City Circuit Court Adult Drug Treatment Court and Felony Diversion Initiative: Outcome and Cost Evaluation-Final Report*. Portland, OR: NPC Research, 2009.

Mackin, Juliette R., Lisa M. Lucas, Callie H. Lambarth, Mark S. Waller, Theresa Allen Herrera, Shannon M. Carey, and Michael W. Finigan. *Howard County District Court Drug Treatment Court Program Outcome and Cost Evaluation*. Portland, OR: NPC Research, 2010.

Mackin, Juliette R., Lisa M. Lucas, Callie H. Lambarth, Mark S. Waller, Theresa Allen Herrera, Shannon M. Carey, and Michael W. Finigan. *Montgomery County Adult Drug Court Program Outcome and Cost Evaluation*. Portland, OR: NPC Research, 2010.

Mackin, Juliette R., Lisa M. Lucas, Callie H. Lambarth, Mark S. Waller, Theresa Allen Herrera, Shannon M. Carey, and Michael W. Finigan. *Wicomico County Circuit Court Adult Drug Treatment Court Program Outcome and Cost Evaluation*. Portland, OR: NPC Research, 2009.

Mackin, Juliette R., Lisa M. Lucas, Callie H. Lambarth, Mark S. Waller, Judy M. Weller, Jennifer A. Aborn, Robert Linhares, Theresa L. Allen, Shannon M. Carey, and Michael W. Finigan. *Baltimore City District Court Adult Drug Treatment Court: 10-Year Outcome and Cost Evaluation*. Portland, OR: NPC Research, 2009.

Marchand, Gwen, Mark Waller, and Shannon M. Carey. *Barry County Adult Drug Court Outcome and Cost Evaluation-Final Report*. Portland, OR: NPC Research, 2006.

Marchand, Gwen, Mark Waller, and Shannon M. Carey. *Kalamazoo County Adult Drug Treatment Court Outcome and Cost Evaluation-Final Report*. Portland, OR: NPC Research, 2006.

Marinelli-Casey, Patricia, Rachel Gonzales, Maureen Hillhouse, Alfonso Ang, Joan Zweben, Judith Cohen, Peggy Fulton Hora, and Richard A. Rawson. "Drug court treatment for methamphetamine dependence: Treatment response and posttreatment outcomes." *Journal of Substance Abuse Treatment*, 34(2) (March 2008): 242-248.

Mitchell, Ojmarrh, and Adele Harrell. "Evaluation of the Breaking the Cycle Demonstration Project: Jacksonville, FL and Tacoma, WA." *Journal of Drug Issues*, 36(1) (Winter 2006): 97-118.

Piper, R. K., and Cassia Spohn. *Cost/Benefit Analysis of the Douglas County Drug Court*. Omaha, NE: University of Nebraska at Omaha, 2004.

Rhodes, William, Ryan Kling, and Michael Shively. *Suffolk County Drug Court Evaluation*. Abt. Associates, Inc., 2006.

Rhyne, Charlene. *Clean Court Outcome Study*. Portland, OR: Multnomah County Department of Community Justice, 2004.

Rossman, S., M. Rempel, J. Roman, et.al. *The Multi-Site Adult Drug Court Evaluation: The Impact of Drug Courts*. Washington, D.C.: Urban Institute, 2011.

Shaffer, Deborah K., Kristin Bechtel, and Edward J. Latessa. *Evaluation of Ohio's Drug Courts: A Cost Benefit Analysis*. Cincinnati, OH: Center for Criminal Justice Research, University of Cincinnati, 2005.

Wilson, David B., Ojmarrh Mitchell, and Doris L. Mackenzie. "A systematic review of drug court effects on recidivism." *Journal of Experimental Criminology,* 2(4) (2006): 459-487.

Zarkin, Gary A., Lara J. Dunlap, Steven Belenko, and Paul A. Dynia. "A Benefit-Cost Analysis of the Kings County District Attorney's Office Drug Treatment Alternative to Prison (DTAP) Program." *Justice Research and Policy*, 7(1) (2005).

End Notes

[1] The types of drug courts include adult drug courts, juvenile drug courts, family drug courts, tribal drug courts, designated Driving Under the Influence (DUI) courts, campus drug courts, reentry drug courts, federal reentry drug courts, veterans drug courts, and co-occurring disorder courts—for offenders with mental health and substance addiction issues.

[2] The Adult Drug Court Discretionary Grant Program was originally authorized under Title V of the Violent Crime Control and Law Enforcement Act of 1994, Pub. L. No. 103-322, 108 Stat. 1796,1955-59, and subsequently reauthorized by Title II of the 21st Century Department of Justice Appropriations Authorization Act, Pub L. No. 107-273, § 2301, 116 Stat. 1758, 1794-99 (2002) (codified at 42 U.S.C. §§ 3797u- u-8). Drug court programs have also received funding from other federal sources, and state and local governments.

[3] BJA's grant solicitation states that to assist DOJ in fulfilling its obligation under GPRA, grantees must provide certain requested data. GPRA was intended to address several broad purposes, including, among other things, improving federal program effectiveness, accountability, and service delivery; and enhancing congressional decision making by providing more objective information on program performance.

[4] GAO, Drug Courts: Better DOJ Data Collection and Evaluation Efforts Needed to Measure Impact of Drug Court Programs, GAO-02-434 (Washington, D.C.: Apr. 18, 2002).

[5] We use the term recidivism to refer generally to the act of committing new criminal offenses after having been arrested or convicted of a crime.

[6] GAO, Drug Courts: Evidence Indicates Recidivism Reductions and Mixed Results for Other Outcomes, GAO-05-219 (Washington, D.C.: Feb. 25, 2005).

[7] Fair Sentencing Act of 2010, Pub. L. No. 111-220, § 9, 124 Stat. 2372, 2374-75.

[8] Grantees are defined as states, state courts, local courts, units of local government, and Indian tribal governments acting directly or through an agreement with other public or private entities that receive funding under the drug court program. 42 U.S.C. § 3797u(a).

[9] GAO, Standards for Internal Control in the Federal Government, GAO-AIMD-00-21.3.1 (Washington, D.C.: November 1999).

[10] GAO, Tax Administration: IRS Needs to Further Refine Its Tax Season Performance Measures, GAO-03-143, (Washington, D.C.: November 2002); and GAO, Recovery Act: Department of Justice Could Better Assess Justice Assistance Grant Program Impact, GAO-11-87 (Washington, D.C.: October 2010).

[11] In February 2005, we studied evaluations of drug court programs that were published from May 1997 through January 2004.

[12] NIJ is the research, development, and evaluation agency of DOJ.

[13] NADCP is a national membership and advocacy organization of drug court professionals that provides for the collection and dissemination of information, technical assistance, and mutual support to association members.

[14] 42 U.S.C. §§ 3797u- u-8. Drug courts funded by BJA are required to involve mandatory periodic drug testing, graduated sanctions for participants who fail drug tests, and continuing judicial supervision over offenders, among other requirements. Id. Federal drug court grants have a matching requirement. Drug court grants are not permitted to cover more than 75 percent of the total costs of the project being funded. Grant applicants are required to identify a nonfederal source of 25 percent of the program's cost with cash or in-kind services, or some combination of both. 42 U.S.C. § 3797u-5.

[15] This joint program offers grantees the opportunity to design a comprehensive strategy for enhancing drug court capacity while accessing both criminal justice and substance-abuse treatment funds under a single grant application. These grants are authorized under section 509 of the Public Health Service Act, as amended (42 U.S.C. § 290bb-2) to provide Adult Treatment Drug Court grants.

[16] The appropriation amounts include adult drug courts, juvenile drug court programs, training and technical assistance, and other related expenses, among other things.

[17] For fiscal year 2011, the number of Adult Drug Court Discretionary Grant Program grantee awards and award amounts were not available at the time of our review.

[18] The average Adult Drug Court Discretionary Grant Program award amount totals ranged from $122,000 in fiscal year 2006 to $267,000 in fiscal year 2010.

[19] GAO-05-219.

[20] See Jeff Latimer, Jeff, Kelly Morton-Bourgon, and Jo-Anne Chrétien. A Meta-Analytic Examination of Drug Treatment Courts: Do they Reduce Recidivism? (Ottawa, Ontario:

Department of Justice Canada, 2006), 12. Christopher T. Lowenkamp, Alexander M. Holsinger, Edward J. Latessa. "Are drug courts effective: A meta-analytic review," Journal of Community Corrections. (Fall 2005), 8, 9, 28. David B. Wilson, Ojmarrh Mitchell, and Doris L. Mackenzie. "A systematic review of drug court effects on recidivism." Journal of Experimental Criminology, 2(4) (2006), 468-469.

[21] BJA officials stated that its Policy, Programs, and Planning Offices participate in the GrantStat reviews.

[22] According to BJA officials, the contactor provides a range of data collection, technical assistance, analytical, and research services to BJA and its grantees. This includes developing and maintaining the PMT and providing a user support help desk and formal training to grantees regarding their reporting requirements. In addition, contractor analysts review, analyze, and report on BJA grantees' performance data to BJA.

[23] See appendix VI for more information regarding the 10 key components.

[24] GAO, Managing For Results: Enhancing Agency Use of Performance Information for Management Decision Making, GAO-05-927 (Washington, D.C.: Sept. 9, 2005).

[25] GAO, Justice: A Time Frame for Enhancing Grant Monitoring Documentation and Verification of Data Quality Would Help Improve Accountability and Resource Allocation Decisions, GAO-09-850R (Washington, DC: September 2009) and GAO, Performance Measurement and Evaluation: Definitions and Relationships, GAO-05-739SP (Washington, DC: May 2005).

[26] GAO, Drug Control: DOD Needs to Improve Its Performance Measurement System to Better Manage and Oversee Its Counternarcotics Activities, GAO-10-835 (Washington, D.C.: July 2010).

[27] We identified the first four management activities in table 1 as relevant from governmentwide surveys of federal managers that GAO conducted in 1997, 2000, and 2003. See GAO-05-927. The remaining two activities we identified, in part, by reviewing performance management literature. BJA staff confirmed each of these six to be relevant to managing the drug court program.

[28] The technical assistance providers included: American University, Tribal Law and Policy Institute, Center for Court Innovation, the National Association of Drug Court Professionals, the Office of Management and Budget, and the National Center for State Courts.

[29] BJA reported that DOJ stakeholders consulted included staff from NIJ, OJP, DOJ's Policy, Management, and Planning Branch, DOJ's Chief Financial Officer, the Office of Juvenile Justice and Delinquency Programs, and BJA's Director.

[30] GAO, Information Security: Concerted Effort needed to Improve Federal Performance Measures, GAO-09-617 (Washington, D.C.: September 2009); GAO, Results-Oriented Cultures: Creating a Clear Linkage between Individual Performance and Organizational Success, GAO 03-488 (Washington, D.C.: March 2003); and GAO, Managing for Results: Measuring Program Results That Are Under Limited Federal Control GAO/GGD-99-16, (Washington, D.C.: December 1998).

[31] These attributes are clarity, reliability, linkage to strategic goals, objectivity, and measurable targets. See GAO, Tax Administration: IRS Needs to Further Refine Its Tax Filing Season Performance Measures, GAO-03-143, (Washington, D.C.: November 2002); and GAO, Recovery Act: Department of Justice Could Better Assess Justice Assistance Grant Program Impact, GAO-11-87 (Washington, D.C.: October 2010).

[32] GAO, Grants Management: Enhancing Performance Accountability Provisions Could Lead to Better Results, GAO-06-1046 (Washington, D.C.: September 2006).

[33] GAO-09-850R; GAO, Performance Plans: Selected Approaches for Verification and Validation of Agency Performance Information, GAO/GGD-99-139 (Washington, D.C.: July, 1999).

[34] GAO-05-927.

[35] GAO/GGD-99-139.

[36] Theodore H. Poister, Measuring Performance in Public and Nonprofit Organizations. The Jossey-Bass Non-Profit and Public Management Series (San Francisco: Jossey- Bass, 2003).

[37] GAO-AIMD-00-21.3.1.

[38] We report findings to be statistically significant only if they were significant at the 95- percent, or greater, level of statistical significance, even though some studies reported findings to be statistically significant at the 90-percent level. In general, the evaluations we reviewed reported differences in overall rearrest rates—that is, the percentage of a group rearrested for any new offense in a given period of time—although some evaluations reported differences in the number of re-arrests or the relative odds of re-arrest. Of the 32 programs reviewed, 31 showed lower recidivism for drug court program participants, and for 18 of these programs, the differences were statistically significant. The findings for the remaining 13 programs were either not statistically significant or the significance of their findings was not reported.

[39] It is important to note that the studies we reviewed did not include treatments other than drug court; for example, they did not measure the relative effectiveness of drug treatment programs administered outside of a drug court.

[40] These percentages were adjusted for differences in the baseline characteristics of the individuals in the two groups compared as well as differences in the baseline characteristics of the programs they were in.

[41] The range of percentage differences for re-arrest rates was narrower for higher quality studies as a group than for lower quality studies, and the differences for higher quality studies did not range as high.

[42] We are reporting on the eight programs for which drug -relapse data from drug court participants were compared with a comparison group. Evaluations of other programs included information on drug-relapse only for drug court participants.

[43] The estimate of $6,208 reflects the hierarchical modeling used in the MADCE study. However, according to NIJ officials, the estimated net benefits could be as low as $5,680, under different assumptions.

End Notes for Appendix I

[1] GAO tracks recommendations for implementation and has closed these as either being fully or partially implemented.

[2] GAO-02-434.

End Notes for Appendix II

[1] The Urban Institute is a nonpartisan economic and social policy research organization. The Center for Court Innovation functions as the independent research and development arm for

the New York State court system and provides criminal justice consulting services to jurisdictions outside New York. The Research Triangle Institute is an independent, nonprofit institute that provides research, development, and technical services to government and commercial clients.

[2] Numbers, percentages, and differences in the foregoing and following bullets, are adjusted (or estimated), as opposed to raw (or observed) numbers, percentages or differences; that is, they were obtained by the MADCE researchers from statistical models that estimated them after adjusting for differences in the baseline characteristics of the individuals in the two groups compared as well as differences in the baseline characteristics of the programs they were in.

[3] Propensity score adjustments are a statistical approach to control for baseline differences between the drug court and comparison groups and to correct for attrition and selection biases by effectively giving greater weight to underrepresented categories of offenders and lesser weight to overrepresented categories of offenders. Hierarchical linear models are used to take account of the nesting—or clustering—of participants within the different sites. These statistical adjustments were necessary as a result of baseline differences between specific drug court and comparison groups and the specific individuals in them, and because of the attrition that occurred in both the drug offender and comparison samples over time.

[4] The estimate of $6,208 reflects the hierarchical modeling used in the MADCE study. However, according to NIJ officials, the estimated net benefits could be as low as $5,680, under different assumptions.

[5] Office of Management and Budget, Circular A-94 Guidelines and Discount Rates for Benefit-Cost Analysis of Federal Programs (Washington, D.C.: 1992.) p 4.

End Notes for Appendix III

[1] Grantees are defined as states, state courts, local courts, units of local government, and Indian tribal governments acting directly or through an agreement with other public or private entities that receive funding under the drug court program. 42 U.S.C. § 3797u(a).

[2] GAO, Standards for Internal Control in the Federal Government, GAO-AIMD-00-21.3.1 (Washington, D.C.: November, 1999).

[3] The management activities include: (1) setting program priorities; (2) allocating resources; (3) adopting new program approaches or changing work processes; (4) identifying and sharing with stakeholders more effective processes and approaches to program implementation; (5) setting expectations for grantees; and (6) monitoring grantee performance.

[4] GAO, Tax Administration: IRS Needs to Further Refine Its Tax Filing Season Performance Measures, GAO-03-143, (Washington, D.C.: November 2002); and GAO, Recovery Act: Department of Justice Could Better Assess Justice Assistance Grant Program Impact, GAO-11-87 (Washington, D.C.: October 2010).

[5] In February 2005, we studied evaluations of drug court programs that were published from May 1997 through January 2004.

[6] We searched the ERIC, Biosis Previews, Social Scisearch, Gale Group Magazine Database, Gale Group Health & Wellness Database, Gale Group Legal Resource Index, Wilson Social Science Abstracts, and Periodical Abstracts PlusText.

[7] Prior GAO reports included, GAO, Drug Courts: Information on a New Approach to Address Drug-Related Crime, GAO/GGD-95-159BR (Washington, D.C.: May 22, 1995); GAO,

Drug Courts: Overview of Growth, Characteristics, and Results, GAO/GGD-97-106 (Washington, D.C.: July 31, 1997); and GAO, Drug Courts: Better DOJ Data Collection and Evaluation Efforts Needed to Measure Impact of Drug Court Programs, GAO-02-434 (Washington, D.C.: Apr. 18, 2002); GAO, Adult Drug Courts: Evidence Indicates Recidivism Reductions and Mixed Results for Other Outcomes, GAO-05-219 (Washington, D.C.: Feb. 28, 2005).

[8] A process evaluation assesses the extent to which a program is operating as it was intended. It typically assesses program activities' conformance to statutory and regulatory requirements, program design, and professional standards or customer expectations.

[9] An experimental design is one in which eligible offenders were randomly assigned to different programs. A quasi-experimental design is one in which (1) all drug-court program participants were compared with an appropriate group of comparable offenders who did not participate in the drug court program, and (2) appropriate statistical methods were used to adjust, or control, for group differences.

[10] Some studies reported results that were aggregated from multiple drug court programs.

[11] For a summary of how drug court studies have addressed selection bias in the past, see GAO-05-219, p 16-24.

[12] GAO-05-219, p 27.

End Notes for Appendix IV

[1] Drug courts funded by BJA are required to involve mandatory periodic drug testing, graduated sanctions for participants who fail drug tests, and continuing judicial supervision over offenders, among other requirements. 42 U.S.C. §§ 3797u- u-8.

In: Adult Drug Courts
Editor: Joan B. Calahan
ISBN: 978-1-62417-163-5

Chapter 2

DRUG COURTS*

United States Department of Justice

BACKGROUND

Drug courts are specialized court docket programs that target criminal defendants and offenders, juvenile offenders, and parents with pending child welfare cases who have alcohol and other drug dependency problems. Although drug courts vary in target population and resources, programs are generally managed by a multidisciplinary team including judges, prosecutors, defense attorneys, community corrections, social workers and treatment service professionals. Support from stakeholders representing law enforcement, the family and the community is encouraged through participation in hearings, programming and events like graduation.

Adult drug courts employ a program designed to reduce drug use relapse and criminal recidivism among defendants and offenders through risk and needs assessment, judicial interaction, monitoring and supervision, graduated sanctions and incentives, treatment and various rehabilitation services.

Juvenile drug courts apply a similar program model that is tailored to the needs of juvenile offenders. These programs provide youth and their families with counseling, education and other services to: promote immediate intervention, treatment and structure; improve level of functioning; address

---

* This is an edited, reformatted and augmented version of the U.S. Department of Justice, Office of Justice Programs publication, dated May 2012.

problems that may contribute to drug use; build skills that increase their ability to lead drug- and crime-free lives; strengthen the family's capacity to offer structure and guidance; and promote accountability for all involved.

Family drug courts emphasize treatment for parents with substance use disorders to aid in the reunification and stabilization of families affected by parental drug use. These programs apply the adult drug court model to cases entering the child welfare system that include allegations of child abuse or neglect in which substance abuse is identified as a contributing factor. Program goals include: helping the parent to become emotionally, financially and personally self-sufficient; promoting the development of parenting and coping skills adequate for serving as an effective parent on a day-to-day basis; and providing services to their children.

Other types of drug courts have emerged to address issues specific to unique populations including tribal, driving while intoxicated (DWI), campus, reentry, veterans and mental health courts.

PROGRAM DEVELOPMENT, RESEARCH AND DISSEMINATION

Through financial grants and other assistance, the *Bureau of Justice Assistance* (BJA) supports building drug court capacity to increase participation among appropriate adult target populations and to maximize criminal justice and treatment resources, such as in partnership with the Substance Abuse and Mental Health Services Administration (SAMHSA) and the Department of Veterans Affairs. BJA provides training and technical assistance through the *National Drug Court Resource Center*, which supports several drug court services.

The *Adult Drug Court Technical Assistance Project* at American University, and the *Statewide Adult Drug Court Training and Technical Assistance Program* at the Center for Court Innovation, deliver onsite and other operations development and implementation services.

The Tribal Law and Policy Institute serves tribal healing to wellness (drug) courts with a *Tribal Drug Court Training and Technical Assistance Program.* The *National Drug Court Institute* (NDCI) reports information updates on drug court activities and delivers an extensive curriculum to drug court professionals through national conferences, regional planning and other training meetings.

The *Office of Juvenile Justice and Delinquency Prevention* (OJJDP) supports juvenile and family drug court programs through financial grants and other assistance, including assessment tool development. In 2007, OJJDP partnered with SAMHSA and the Robert Wood Johnson Foundation to better serve substance-abusing delinquents by developing juvenile drug courts that apply the Reclaiming Futures program model. OJJDP provided funds for an evaluation by the University of Arizona of six *Juvenile Drug Court/ Reclaiming Futures Program* sites. OJJDP started a *Juvenile Drug Courts Mentoring and Support Services Initiative* in 2010, and provides training and technical assistance through the National Council of Juvenile and Family Court Judges and NDCI to juvenile programs, and through the Center for Children and Family Futures to family programs. OJJDP's *Evaluation of Juvenile Drug Court Programs* is a study of nine programs to assess their effectiveness in reducing recidivism and improving youths' social conditions, and to identify the characteristics of youth and programs most associated with successful outcomes.

The *National Institute of Justice* (NIJ) funds research on drug court processes, impact and cost efficiency. One evaluation tracked 10 years of cohorts in the Multnomah County Drug Court and found rearrests were lower 5 years or more later for participants than for comparable drug offenders; however, reductions ranged from 17 percent to 26 percent over cohorts with changes in programming and judge assignments.

NIJ's Multisite Adult Drug Court Evaluation found that programs significantly reduce drug use and criminal offending — both during and after program participation. Compared to traditional case processing and supervision, drug courts have higher investment costs especially in treatment services. However, savings associated with victim and criminal justice system costs are greater due to fewer crimes, rearrests and incarceration. Drug courts that target offenders with high criminogenic risk and high substance abuse treatment need yield the most effective interventions and maximize return on investment. BJA and NIJ's joint *Adult Drug Court Research to Practice (R2P) Initiative* promotes the timely dissemination of information emerging from research on addiction science, substance abuse treatment and drug court programs.

The project awarded to the National Center for State Courts and American University produces webinars, webcasts and other research dissemination to practitioners, policymakers and other stakeholders.

Number and Types of Drug Courts

There are more than 2,600 drug courts across the United States, of which half are adult treatment drug courts.

Adult drug courts are guided by 10 key components (see Defining Drug Courts: The Key Components[1]) and BJA's Seven Program Design Features.[2]

Growing in number are family (329), driving while intoxicated or DWI (192), and other drug courts serving specific needs. Juvenile drug courts have decreased (458).

Juvenile drug courts are guided by 16 strategies; see Juvenile Drug Courts: Strategies in Practice. [3]

Family drug courts are guided by 10 Key Principles for Permanency Planning for Children.[4]

Research Findings

NIJ's Multisite Adult Drug Court Evaluation[5] found:

- Participants reported less criminal activity (40% vs. 53%) and had fewer rearrests (52% vs. 62%) than comparable offenders.
- Participants reported less drug use (56% vs. 76%) and were less likely to test positive (29% vs. 46%) than comparable offenders.
- Treatment investment costs were higher for participants, but with less recidivism, drug courts saved an average of $5,680 to $6,208 per offender overall.

Resources

- BJA Drug Court Discretionary Grant Program https://www. bja.gov/ ProgramDetails. aspx?Program_ID=58
- National Drug Court Resource Center http://ndcrc.org/
- Drug Court Clearinghouse/Adult Technical Assistance Project http://www1.spa.american.edu/justice/ project.php?ID=1
- Statewide Adult Drug Court Training and Technical Assistance Program http://www.drugcourtta.org/

- Tribal Drug Court Training and Technical Assistance Program http://www.tribal-institute.org/lists/ drug_court.htm
- National Drug Court Institute http://www.ndci.org/ndci-home/
- National Council of Juvenile and Family Court Judges http://www.ncjfcj.org/
- Center for Children and Family Futures http://www.cffutures.org/
- Juvenile Drug Courts/Reclaiming Futures Program http://www.ojjdp.gov/programs/ProgSummary.asp?pi=44&ti=&si=&kw=& PreviousPage=ProgResults
- NIJ's Research on Drug Courts http://www.nij.gov/nij/topics/courts/drug-courts/welcome.htm
- Adult Drug Court Research to Practice (R2P) Initiative http://research2practice.org/

End Notes

[1] https://www.ncjrs.gov/pdffiles1/bja/205621.pdf.
[2] http://www.ndcrc.org/content/webinar-seven-program-design-features.
[3] http://www.ncjrs.gov/pdffiles1/bja/197866.pdf.
[4] http://www.ncjfcj.org/sites/default/files/keyprinciples.final_.permplanning. pdf.
[5] http://www.nij.gov/nij/topics/courts/drug-courts/madce.htm.

In: Adult Drug Courts
Editor: Joan B. Calahan

ISBN: 978-1-62417-163-5

Chapter 3

DEFINING DRUG COURTS: THE KEY COMPONENTS*

United States Department of Justice

KEY COMPONENT #1

Drug Courts Integrate Alcohol and Other Drug Treatment Services with Justice System Case Processing

Purpose

The mission of drug courts is to stop the abuse of alcohol and other drugs and related criminal activity. Drug courts promote recovery through a coordinated response to offenders dependent on alcohol and other drugs. Realization of these goals requires a team approach, including cooperation and collaboration of the judges, prosecutors, defense counsel, probation authorities, other corrections personnel, law enforcement, pretrial services agencies, TASC programs, evaluators, an array of local service providers, and the greater community. State-level organizations representing AOD issues, law enforcement and criminal justice, vocational rehabilitation, education, and housing also have important roles to play. The combined energies of these

* This is an edited, reformatted and augmented version of a U.S. Department of Justice, Office of Justice Programs, Bureau of Justice Assistance publication, dated October 2004.

individuals and organizations can assist and encourage defendants to accept help that could change their lives.

The criminal justice system has the unique ability to influence a person shortly after a significant triggering event such as arrest, and thus persuade or compel that person to enter and remain in treatment. Research indicates that a person coerced to enter treatment by the criminal justice system is likely to do as well as one who volunteers.[1]

Drug courts usually employ a multiphased treatment process, generally divided into a stabilization phase, an intensive treatment phase, and a transition phase. The stabilization phase may include a period of AOD detoxification, initial treatment assessment, education, and screening for other needs. The intensive treatment phase typically involves individual and group counseling and other core and adjunctive therapies as they are available (see Key Component #4). The transition phase may emphasize social reintegration, employment and education, housing services, and other aftercare activities.

Performance Benchmarks

1) Initial and ongoing planning is carried out by a broad-based group, including persons representing all aspects of the criminal justice system, the local treatment delivery system, funding agencies, and the local community's other key policymakers.
2) Documents defining the drug court's mission, goals, eligibility criteria, operating procedures, and performance measures are collaboratively developed, reviewed, and agreed upon.
3) Abstinence and law-abiding behavior are the goals, with specific and measurable criteria marking progress. Criteria may include compliance with program requirements, reductions in criminal behavior and AOD use, participation in treatment, restitution to the victim or to the community, and declining incidence of AOD use.
4) The court and treatment providers maintain ongoing communication, including frequent exchanges of timely and accurate information about the individual participant's overall program performance.[2]
5) The judge plays an active role in the treatment process, including frequently reviewing treatment progress. The judge responds to each participant's positive efforts as well as to noncompliant behavior.
6) Interdisciplinary education is provided for every person involved in drug court operations to develop a shared understanding of the values, goals, and operating procedures of both the treatment and justice system components.

7) Mechanisms for sharing decisionmaking and resolving conflicts among drug court team members, such as multidisciplinary committees, are established to ensure professional integrity.

KEY COMPONENT #2

Using a Nonadversarial Approach, Prosecution and Defense Counsel Promote Public Safety While Protecting Participants' Due Process Rights

Purpose

To facilitate an individual's progress in treatment, the prosecutor and defense counsel must shed their traditional adversarial courtroom relationship and work together as a team. Once a defendant is accepted into the drug court program, the team's focus is on the participant's recovery and law-abiding behavior—not on the merits of the pending case. The responsibility of the prosecuting attorney is to protect the public's safety by ensuring that each candidate is appropriate for the program and complies with all drug court requirements. The responsibility of the defense counsel is to protect the participant's due process rights while encouraging full participation. Both the prosecuting attorney and the defense counsel play important roles in the court's coordinated strategy for responding to noncompliance.

Performance Benchmarks

1) Prosecutors and defense counsel participate in the design of screening, eligibility, and case-processing policies and procedures to guarantee that due process rights and public safety needs are served.
2) For consistency and stability in the early stages of drug court operations, the judge, prosecutor, and court-appointed defense counsel should be assigned to the drug court for a sufficient period of time to build a sense of teamwork and to reinforce a nonadversarial atmosphere.
3) The prosecuting attorney:
   - Li Reviews the case and determines if the defendant is eligible for the drug court program.
   - Li Files all necessary legal documents.

- Li Participates in a coordinated strategy for responding to positive drug tests and other instances of noncompliance.
- Li Agrees that a positive drug test or open court admission of drug possession or use will not result in the filing of additional drug charges based on that admission.
- Li Makes decisions regarding the participant's continued enrollment in the program based on performance in treatment rather than on legal aspects of the case, barring additional criminal behavior.

4) The defense counsel:
   - Reviews the arrest warrant, affidavits, charging document, and other relevant information, and reviews all program documents (e.g., waivers, written agreements).
   - governing participation, the consequences of abiding or failing to abide by the rules, and how participating or not participating in the drug court will affect his or her interests.
   - Explains all of the rights that the defendant will temporarily or permanently relinquish.
   - Gives advice on alternative courses of action, including legal and treatment alternatives available outside the drug court program, and discusses with the defendant the long-term benefits of sobriety and a drug-free life.
   - Explains that because criminal prosecution for admitting to AOD use in open court will not be invoked, the defendant is encouraged to be truthful with the judge and with treatment staff, and informs the participant that he or she will be expected to speak directly to the judge, not through an attorney.

KEY COMPONENT #3

Eligible Participants are Identified Early and Promptly Placed in the Drug Court Program

Purpose

Arrest can be a traumatic event in a person's life. It creates an immediate crisis and can force substance abusing behavior into the open, making denial difficult. The period immediately after an arrest, or after apprehension for a probation violation, provides a critical window of opportunity for intervening and introducing the value of AOD treatment. Judicial action, taken promptly after arrest, capitalizes on the crisis nature of the arrest and booking process.

Rapid and effective action also increases public confidence in the criminal justice system. Moreover, incorporating AOD concerns into the case disposition process can be a key element in strategies to link criminal justice and AOD treatment systems overall.

Performance Benchmarks

1) Eligibility screening is based on established written criteria. Criminal justice officials or others (e.g., pretrial services, probation, TASC) are designated to screen cases and identify potential drug court participants.
2) Eligible participants for drug court are promptly advised about program requirements and the relative merits of participating.
3) Trained professionals screen drug court-eligible individuals for AOD problems and suitability for treatment.
4) Initial appearance before the drug court judge occurs immediately after arrest or apprehension to ensure program participation.
5) The court requires that eligible participants enroll in AOD treatment services immediately.

KEY COMPONENT #4

Drug Courts Provide Access to a Continuum of Alcohol, Drug, and Other Related Treatment and Rehabilitation Services

Purpose

The origins and patterns of AOD problems are complex and unique to each individual. They are influenced by a variety of accumulated social and cultural experiences. If treatment for AOD is to be effective, it must also call on the resources of primary health and mental health care and make use of social and other support services.[3]

In a drug court, the treatment experience begins in the courtroom and continues through the participant's drug court involvement. In other words, drug court is a comprehensive therapeutic experience, only part of which takes place in a designated treatment setting. The treatment and criminal justice professionals are members of the therapeutic team.

The therapeutic team (treatment providers, the judge, lawyers, case managers, supervisors, and other program staff) should maintain frequent, regular communication to provide timely reporting of a participant's progress and to ensure that responses to compliance and noncompliance are swift and coordinated. Procedures for reporting progress should be clearly defined in the drug court's operating documents.

While primarily concerned with criminal activity and AOD use, the drug court team also needs to consider co-occurring problems such as mental illness, primary medical problems, HIV and sexually-transmitted diseases, homelessness; basic educational deficits, unemployment and poor job preparation; spouse and family troubles—especially domestic violence—and the long-term effects of childhood physical and sexual abuse. If not addressed, these factors will impair an individual's success in treatment and will compromise compliance with program requirements. Co-occurring factors should be considered in treatment planning. In addition, treatment services must be relevant to the ethnicity, gender, age, and other characteristics of the participants.

Longitudinal studies have consistently documented the effectiveness of AOD treatment in reducing criminal recidivism and AOD use.[4] A study commissioned by the Office of National Drug Control Policy found AOD treatment is significantly more cost-effective than domestic law enforcement, interdiction, or "source-country control" in reducing drug use in the United States.[5] Research indicates that the length of time an offender spends in treatment is related to the level of AOD abuse and criminal justice involvement.[6] A comprehensive study conducted by the State of California indicates that AOD treatment provides a $7 return for every $1 spent on treatment. The study found that outpatient treatment is the most cost-effective approach, although residential treatment, sober living houses, and methadone maintenance are also cost-effective.[7] Comprehensive studies conducted in California[8] and Oregon[9] found that positive outcomes associated with AOD treatment are sustained for several years following completion of treatment.

For the many communities that do not have adequate treatment resources, drug courts can provide leadership to increase treatment options and enrich the availability of support services. Some drug courts have found creative ways to access services, such as implementing treatment readiness programs for participants who are on waiting lists for comprehensive treatment programs. In some jurisdictions, drug courts have established their own treatment programs where none existed. Other drug courts have made use of pretrial, probation, and public health treatment services.

Performance Benchmarks

1) Individuals are initially screened and thereafter periodically assessed by both court and treatment personnel to ensure that treatment services and individuals are suitably matched:
   - Li An assessment at treatment entry, while useful as a baseline, provides a time specific "snapshot" of a person's needs and may be based on limited or unreliable information. Ongoing assessment is necessary to monitor progress, to change the treatment plan as necessary, and to identify relapse cues.
   - Li If various levels of treatment are available, participants are matched to programs according to their specific needs. Guidelines for placement at various levels should be developed.
   - Li Screening for infectious diseases and health referrals occurs at an early stage.
2) Treatment services are comprehensive:
   - Services should be available to meet the needs of each participant.
   - Treatment services may include, but are not limited to, group counseling; individual and family counseling; relapse prevention; 12-step self-help groups; preventive and primary medical care; general health education; medical detoxification; acupuncture for detoxification, for control of craving, and to make people more amenable to treatment; domestic violence programs; batterers' treatment; and treatment for the long-term effects of childhood physical and sexual abuse.
   - Other services may include housing; educational and vocational training; legal, money management, and other social service needs; cognitive behavioral therapy to address criminal thinking patterns; anger management; transitional housing; social and athletic activities; and meditation or other techniques to promote relaxation and self-control.
   - Specialized services should be considered for participants with co-occurring AOD problems and mental health disorders. Drug courts should establish linkages with mental health providers to furnish services (e.g., medication monitoring, acute care) for participants with co-occurring disorders. Flexibility (e.g., in duration of treatment phases) is essential in designing drug court services for participants with mental health problems.

- Treatment programs or program components are designed to address the particular treatment issues of women and other special populations.
- Treatment is available in a number of settings, including detoxification, acute residential, day treatment, outpatient, and sober living residences.
- Clinical case management services are available to provide ongoing assessment of participant progress and needs, to coordinate referrals to services in addition to primary treatment, to provide structure and support for individuals who typically have difficulty using services even when they are available, and to ensure communication between the court and the various service providers.

3) Treatment services are accessible:
   - Accommodations are made for persons with physical disabilities, for those not fluent in English, for those needing child care, and/or for persons with limited literacy.
   - Treatment facilities are accessible by public transportation, when possible.
4) Funding for treatment is adequate, stable, and dedicated to the drug court:
   - To ensure that services are immediately available throughout the participant's treatment, agreements are made between courts and treatment providers. These agreements are based on firm budgetary and service delivery commitments.
   - Diverse treatment funding strategies are developed based on both government and private sources at national, State, and local levels.
   - Health care delivered through managed care organizations is encouraged to provide resources for the AOD treatment of member participants.
   - Payment of fees, fines, and restitution is part of treatment.
   - Fee schedules are commensurate with an individual's ability to pay. However, no one should be turned away solely because of an inability to pay.
5) Treatment services have quality controls:
   - Direct service providers are certified or licensed where required, or otherwise demonstrate proficiency according to accepted professional standards.

- Education, training, and ongoing clinical supervision are provided to treatment staff.

6) Treatment agencies are accountable:
   - Treatment agencies give the court accurate and timely information about a participant's progress. Information exchange complies with the provisions of 42 CFR, Part 2 (the Federal regulations governing confidentiality of AOD abuse patient records) and with applicable State statutes.
   - Responses to progress and noncompliance are incorporated into the treatment protocols.
7) Treatment designs and delivery systems are sensitive and relevant to issues of race, culture, religion, gender, age, ethnicity, and sexual orientation.

KEY COMPONENT #5

Abstinence Is Monitored by Frequent Alcohol and Other Drug Testing. Purpose

Frequent court-ordered AOD testing is essential. An accurate testing program is the most objective and efficient way to establish a framework for accountability and to gauge each participant's progress. Modern technology offers highly reliable testing to determine if an individual has recently used specific drugs. Further, it is commonly recognized that alcohol use frequently contributes to relapse among individuals whose primary drug of choice is not alcohol.

AOD testing results are objective measures of treatment effectiveness, as well as a source of important information for periodic review of treatment progress. AOD testing helps shape the ongoing interaction between the court and each participant. Timely and accurate test results promote frankness and honesty among all parties.

AOD testing is central to the drug court's monitoring of participant compliance. It is both objective and cost-effective. It gives the participant immediate information about his or her own progress, making the participant active and involved in the treatment process rather than a passive recipient of services.

Performance Benchmarks

1) AOD testing policies and procedures are based on established and tested guidelines, such as those established by the American Probation and Parole Association. Contracted laboratories analyzing urine or other samples should also be held to established standards.
2) Testing may be administered randomly or at scheduled intervals, but occurs no less than twice a week during the first several months of an individual's enrollment. Frequency thereafter will vary depending on participant progress.
3) The scope of testing is sufficiently broad to detect the participant's primary drug of choice as well as other potential drugs of abuse, including alcohol.
4) The drug-testing procedure must be certain. Elements contributing to the reliability and validity of a urinalysis testing process include, but are not limited to:
   - Li Direct observation of urine sample collection.
   - Li Verification temperature and measurement of creatinine levels to determine the extent of water loading.
   - Li Specific, detailed, written procedures regarding all aspects of urine sample collection, sample analysis, and result reporting.
   - Li A documented chain of custody for each sample collected.
   - Quality control and quality assurance procedures for ensuring the integrity of the process.
   - Procedures for verifying accuracy when drug test results are contested.
5) Ideally, test results are available and communicated to the court and the participant within one day. The drug court functions best when it can respond immediately to noncompliance; the time between sample collection and availability of results should be short.
6) The court is immediately notified when a participant has tested positive, has failed to submit to AOD testing, has submitted the sample of another, or has adulterated a sample.
7) The coordinated strategy for responding to noncompliance includes prompt responses to positive tests, missed tests, and fraudulent tests.
8) Participants should be abstinent for a substantial period of time prior to program graduation.

KEY COMPONENT #6

A Coordinated Strategy Governs Drug Court Responses to Participants' Compliance

Purpose

An established principle of AOD treatment is that addiction is a chronic, relapsing condition. A pattern of decreasing frequency of use before sustained abstinence from alcohol and other drugs is common. Becoming sober or drug free is a learning experience, and each relapse to AOD use may teach something about the recovery process.

Implemented in the early stages of treatment and emphasized throughout, therapeutic strategies aimed at preventing the return to AOD use help participants learn to manage their ambivalence toward recovery, identify situations that stimulate AOD cravings, and develop skills to cope with high-risk situations. Eventually, participants learn to manage cravings, avoid or deal more effectively with high-risk situations, and maintain sobriety for increasing lengths of time.

Abstinence and public safety are the ultimate goals of drug courts, many participants exhibit a pattern of positive urine tests within the first several months following admission. Because AOD problems take a long time to develop and because many factors contribute to drug use and dependency, it is rare that an individual ceases AOD use as soon as he or she enrolls in treatment. Even after a period of sustained abstinence, it is common for individuals to occasionally test positive.

Although drug courts recognize that individuals have a tendency to relapse, continuing AOD use is not condoned. Drug courts impose appropriate responses for continuing AOD use. Responses increase in severity for continued failure to abstain.

A participant's progress through the drug court experience is measured by his or her compliance with the treatment regimen. Certainly cessation of drug use is the ultimate goal of drug court treatment. However, there is value in recognizing incremental progress toward the goal, such as showing up at all required court appearances, regularly arriving at the treatment program on time, attending and fully participating in the treatment sessions, cooperating with treatment staff, and submitting to regular AOD testing.

Drug courts must reward cooperation as well as respond to noncompliance. Small rewards for incremental successes have an important effect on a participant's sense of purpose and accomplishment. Praise from the drug court judge for regular attendance or for a period of clean drug tests, encouragement from the treatment staff or the judge at particularly difficult times, and ceremonies in which tokens of accomplishment are awarded in open court for completing a particular phase of treatment are all small but very important rewards that bolster confidence and give inspiration to continue.

Drug courts establish a coordinated strategy, including a continuum of responses, to continuing drug use and other noncompliant behavior. A coordinated strategy can provide a common operating plan for treatment providers and other drug court personnel. The criminal justice system representatives and the treatment providers develop a series of complementary, measured responses that will encourage compliance. A written copy of these responses, given to participants during the orientation period, emphasizes the predictability, certainty, and swiftness of their application.

Performance Benchmarks

1) Treatment providers, the judge, and other program staff maintain frequent, regular communication to provide timely reporting of progress and noncompliance and to enable the court to respond immediately. Procedures for reporting noncompliance are clearly defined in the drug court's operating documents.
2) Responses to compliance and noncompliance are explained verbally and provided in writing to drug court participants before their orientation. Periodic reminders are given throughout the treatment process.
3) The responses for compliance vary in intensity:
   - Li Encouragement and praise from the bench.
   - Li Ceremonies and tokens of progress, including advancement to the next treatment phase.
   - Li Reduced supervision.
   - Li Decreased frequency of court appearances.
   - Li Reduced fines or fees.
   - Li Dismissal of criminal charges or reduction in the term of probation.
   - Li Reduced or suspended incarceration.
   - Li Graduation.
4) Responses to or sanctions for noncompliance might include:
   - Li Warnings and admonishment from the bench in open court.
   - Li Demotion to earlier program phases.

- Li Increased frequency of testing and court appearances.
- Li Confinement in the courtroom or jury box.
- Li Increased monitoring and/or treatment intensity.
- Li Fines.
- Li Required community service or work programs.
- Li Escalating periods of jail confinement (however, drug court participants remanded to jail should receive AOD treatment services while confined).
- Li Termination from the program and reinstatement of regular court processing.

KEY COMPONENT #7

Ongoing Judicial Interaction with Each Drug Court Participant Is Essential

Purpose

The judge is the leader of the drug court team, linking participants to AOD treatment and to the criminal justice system. This active, supervising relationship, maintained throughout treatment, increases the likelihood that a participant will remain in treatment and improves the chances for sobriety and law-abiding behavior.

Ongoing judicial supervision also communicates to participants—often for the first time—that someone in authority cares about them and is closely watching what they do.

Drug courts require judges to step beyond their traditionally independent and objective arbiter roles and develop new expertise. The structure of the drug court allows for early and frequent judicial intervention. A drug court judge must be prepared to encourage appropriate behavior and to discourage and penalize inappropriate behavior.

A drug court judge is knowledgeable about treatment methods and their limitations.

Performance Benchmarks

1. Regular status hearings are used to monitor participant performance:
   - Frequent status hearings during the initial phases of each participant's program establish and reinforce the drug court's

policies, and ensure effective supervision of each drug court participant. Frequent hearings also give the participant a sense of how he or she is doing in relation to others.

- Time between status hearings may be increased or decreased, based on compliance with treatment protocols and progress observed.
- Having a significant number of drug court participants appear at a single session gives the judge the opportunity to educate both the offender at the bench and those waiting as to the benefits of program compliance and consequences for noncompliance.

2. The court applies appropriate incentives and sanctions to match the participant's treatment progress.
3. Payment of fees, fines and/or restitution is part of the participant's treatment. The court supervises such payments and takes into account the participant's financial ability to fulfill these obligations. The court ensures that no one is denied participation in drug courts solely because of on an inability to pay fees, fines, or restitution.

KEY COMPONENT #8

Monitoring and Evaluation Measure The Achievement of Program Goals and Gauge Effectiveness

Purpose

Fundamental to the effective operation of drug courts are coordinated management, monitoring, and evaluation systems. The design and operation of an effective drug court program result from thorough initial planning, clearly defined program goals, and inherent flexibility to make modifications as necessary.

The goals of the program should be described concretely and in measurable terms to provide accountability to funding agencies and policymakers. And, since drug courts will increasingly be asked to demonstrate tangible outcomes and cost-effectiveness, it is critical that the drug court be designed with the ability to gather and manage information for monitoring daily activities, evaluating the quality of services provided, and producing longitudinal evaluations.

Management and monitoring systems provide timely and accurate information about program operations to the drug court's managers, enabling them to keep the program on course, identify developing problems, and make appropriate procedural changes. Clearly defined drug court goals shape the management information system, determine monitoring questions, and suggest methods for finding information to answer them.

Program management provides the information needed for day-to-day operations and for planning, monitoring, and evaluation. Program monitoring provides oversight and periodic measurements of the program's performance against its stated goals and objectives.

Evaluation is the institutional process of gathering and analyzing data to measure the accomplishment of the program's long-term goals. A process evaluation appraises progress in meeting operational and administrative goals (e.g., whether treatment services are implemented as intended). An outcome evaluation assesses the extent to which the program is reaching its long-term goals (e.g., reducing criminal recidivism). An effective design for an outcome evaluation uses a comparison group that does not receive drug court services.

Although evaluation activities are often planned and implemented simultaneously, process evaluation information can be used more quickly in the early stages of drug court implementation. Outcome evaluation should be planned at the beginning of the program as it requires at least a year to compile results, especially if past participants are to be found and interviewed.

Evaluation strategies should reflect the significant coordination and the considerable time required to obtain measurable results. Evaluation studies are useful to everyone, including funding agencies and policymakers who may not be involved in the daily operations of the program. Information and conclusions developed from periodic monitoring reports, process evaluation activities, and longitudinal evaluation studies may be used to modify program procedures, change therapeutic interventions, and make decisions about continuing or expanding the program.

Information for management, monitoring, and evaluation purposes may already exist within the court system and/or in the community treatment or supervision agencies (e.g., criminal justice data bases, psychosocial histories, and formal AOD assessments). Multiple sources of information enhance the credibility and persuasiveness of conclusions drawn from evaluations.

Performance Benchmarks

1. Management, monitoring, and evaluation processes begin with initial planning. As part of the comprehensive planning process, drug court leaders and senior managers should establish specific and measurable goals that define the parameters of data collection and information

management. An evaluator can be an important member of the planning team.

2. Data needed for program monitoring and management can be obtained from records maintained for day-to-day program operations, such as the numbers and general demographics of individuals screened for eligibility; the extent and nature of AOD problems among those assessed for possible participation in the program; and attendance records, progress reports, drug test results, and incidence of criminality among those accepted into the program.
3. Monitoring and management data are assembled in useful formats for regular review by program leaders and managers.
4. Ideally, much of the information needed for monitoring and evaluation is gathered through an automated system that can provide timely and useful reports. If an automated system is not available manual data collection and report preparation can be streamlined. Additional monitoring information may be acquired by observation and through program staff and participant interviews.
5. Automated manual information systems must adhere to written guidelines that protect against unauthorized disclosure of sensitive personal information about individuals.
6. Monitoring reports need to be reviewed at frequent intervals by program leaders and senior managers. They can be used to analyze program operations, gauge effectiveness, modify procedures when necessary, and refine goals.
7. Process evaluation activities should be undertaken throughout the course of the drug court program. This activity is particularly important in the early stages of program implementation.
8. If feasible, a qualified independent evaluator should be selected and given responsibility for developing and conducting an evaluation design and for preparing interim and final reports. If an independent evaluation is unavailable the drug court program designs and implements its own evaluation, based on guidance available through the field:

- Judges, prosecutors, the defense bar, treatment staff, and others design the evaluation collaboratively with the evaluator.
- Ideally, an independent evaluator will help the information systems expert design and implement the management information system.

- The drug court program ensures that the evaluator has access to relevant justice system and treatment information.
- The evaluator maintains continuing contact with the drug court and provides information on a regular basis. Preliminary reports may be reviewed by drug court program personnel and used as the basis for revising goals, policies, and procedures as appropriate.

9. Useful data elements to assist in management and monitoring may include, but are not limited to:
   - The number of defendants screened for program eligibility and the outcome of those initial screenings.
   - The number of persons admitted to the drug court program.
   - Characteristics of program participants, such as age, sex, race/ethnicity, family status, employment status, and educational level; current charges; criminal justice history; AOD treatment or mental health treatment history; medical needs (including detoxification); and nature and severity of AOD problems.
   - Number and characteristics of participants (e.g., duration of treatment involvement, reason for discharge from the program).
   - Number of active cases.
   - Patterns of drug use as measured by drug test results.
   - Aggregate attendance data and general treatment progress measurements.
   - Number and characteristics of persons who graduate or complete treatment successfully.
   - Number and characteristics of persons who do not graduate or complete the program.
   - Number of participants who fail to appear at drug court hearings and number of bench warrants issued for participants.
   - Rearrests during involvement in the drug court program and type of arrest(s).
   - Number, length, and reasons for incarcerations during and subsequent to involvement in the drug court program.
10. When making comparisons for evaluation purposes, drug courts should consider the following groups:
    - Program graduates.
    - Program terminations.
    - Individuals who were referred to, but did not appear for, treatment.
    - Individuals who were not referred for drug court services.

11. At least six months after exiting a drug court program, comparison groups (listed above) should be examined to determine long-term effects of the program. Data elements for follow-up evaluation may include:
    - Criminal behavior/activity.
    - Days spent in custody on all offenses from date of acceptance into the program.
    - AOD use since leaving the program.
    - Changes in job skills and employment status.
    - Changes in literacy and other educational attainments.
    - Changes in physical and mental health.
    - Changes in status of family relationships.
    - Attitudes and perceptions of participation in the program.
    - Use of health care and other social services.
12. Drug court evaluations should consider the use of cost-benefit analysis to examine the economic impact of program services. Important elements of cost-benefit analysis include:
    - Reductions in court costs, including judicial, counsel, and investigative resources. Li Reductions in costs related to law enforcement and corrections.
    - Reductions in health care utilization.
    - Increased economic productivity.

KEY COMPONENT #9

Continuing Interdisciplinary Education Promotes Effective Drug Court Planning, Implementation, and Operations

Purpose

Periodic education and training ensures that the drug court's goals and objectives, as well as policies and procedures, are understood not only by the drug court leaders and senior managers, but also by those indirectly involved in the program. Education and training programs also help maintain a high level of professionalism, provide a forum for solidifying relationships among criminal justice and AOD treatment personnel, and promote a spirit of commitment and collaboration.

All drug court staff should be involved in education and training, even before the first case is heard. Interdisciplinary education exposes criminal justice officials to treatment issues, and treatment staff to criminal justice issues. It also develops shared understandings of the values, goals, and operating procedures of both the treatment and the justice system components. Judges and court personnel typically need to learn about the nature of AOD problems and the theories and practices supporting specific treatment approaches.

Treatment providers typically need to become familiar with criminal justice accountability issues and court operations. All need to understand and comply with drug testing standards and procedures.

For justice system or other officials not directly involved in the program's operations, education provides an overview of the mission, goals, and operating procedures of the drug court.

A simple and effective method of educating new drug court staff is to visit an existing court to observe its operations and ask questions. On-site experience with an operating drug court provides an opportunity for new drug court staff to talk to their peers directly and to see how their particular role functions.

Performance Benchmarks

1. Key personnel have attained a specific level of basic education, as defined in staff training requirements and in the written operating procedures. The operating procedures should also define requirements for the continuing education of each drug court staff member.
2. Attendance at education and training sessions by all drug court personnel is essential. Regional and national drug court training provide critical information on innovative developments across the Nation. Sessions are most productive when drug court personnel attend as a group. Credits for continuing professional education should be offered, when feasible.
3. Continuing education institutionalizes the drug court and moves it beyond its initial identification with the key staff who may have founded the program and nurtured its development.
4. An education syllabus and curriculum are developed, describing the drug court's goals, policies, and procedures. Topics might include:
   - Goals and philosophy of drug courts.
   - he nature of AOD abuse, its treatment and terminology.
   - The dynamics of abstinence and techniques for preventing relapse.

- Responses to relapse and to noncompliance with other program requirements.
- Basic legal requirements of the drug court program and an overview of the local criminal justice system's policies, procedures, and terminology.
- Drug testing standards and procedures.
- Sensitivity to racial, cultural, ethnic, gender, and sexual orientation as they affect the operation of the drug court.
- Interrelationships of co-occurring conditions such as AOD abuse and mental illness (also known as "dual diagnosis").
- Federal, State, and local confidentiality requirements.

KEY COMPONENT #10

Forging Partnerships Among Drug Courts, Public Agencies, and Community-Based Organizations Generates Local Support and Enhances Drug Court Program Effectiveness

Purpose

Because of its unique position in the criminal justice system, a drug court is especially well suited to develop coalitions among private community-based organizations, public criminal justice agencies, and AOD treatment delivery systems. Forming such coalitions expands the continuum of services available to drug court participants and informs the community about drug court concepts. The drug court is a partnership among organizations—public, private, and communitybased—dedicated to a coordinated and cooperative approach to the AOD offender. The drug court fosters systemwide involvement through its commitment to share responsibility and participation of program partners.

As a part of, and as a leader in, the formation and operation of community partnerships, drug courts can help restore public faith in the criminal justice system.

Performance Benchmarks

1. Representatives from the court, community organizations, law enforcement, corrections, prosecution, defense counsel, supervisory

agencies, treatment and rehabilitation providers, educators, health and social service agencies, and the faith community meet regularly to provide guidance and direction to the drug court program.

2. The drug court plays a pivotal role in forming linkages between community groups and the criminal justice system. The linkages are a conduit of information to the public about the drug court, and conversely, from the community to the court about available community services and local problems.
3. Partnerships between drug courts and law enforcement and/or community policing programs can build effective links between the court and offenders in the community.
4. Participation of public and private agencies, as well as community-based organizations, is formalized through a steering committee. The steering committee aids in the acquisition and distribution of resources. An especially effective way for the steering committee to operate is through the formation of a nonprofit corporation structure that includes all the principle drug court partners, provides policy guidance, and acts as a conduit for fundraising and resource acquisition.
5. Drug court programs and services are sensitive to and demonstrate awareness of the populations they serve and the communities in which they operate. Drug courts provide opportunities for community involvement through forums, informational meetings, and other community outreach efforts.
6. The drug court hires a professional staff that reflects the population served, and the drug court provides ongoing cultural competence training.

RESOURCE LIST

Federal Organizations and Agencies Providing Information and Guidance on Drug Courts:

The White House
Office of National Drug Control Policy
(ONDCP)
Executive Office of the President

The White House
1600 Pennsylvania Ave., NW
Washington, DC 20502-0002
Tel: 202/395-6700

U.S. Department of Justice
Bureau of Justice Assistance Office of Justice Programs U.S. Department of Justice 810 Seventh Street, NW Washington, DC 20531 Tel: 202/616-6500
Fax: 202/305-1367
National Criminal Justice Reference Service Tel: 800/851-3420

Federal Agencies and Organizations Providing Information on AOD Treatment:

U.S. Department of Health and Human Services

Alcoholism and Substance Abuse Branch Indian Health Service
5600 Fishers Lane, Room 5A-20
Rockville, MD 20857 Tel: 301/443-7623

Center for Substance Abuse Treatment Substance Abuse and Mental Health Services
Administration, Public Health Service 5515 Security Lane Rockville, MD 20852 Tel: 301/443-5700

National Clearinghouse for Alcohol and Drug
Information
11426 Rockville Pike, Suite 200
Rockville, MD 20852
Tel: 800/729-6686

National Institute on Alcohol and Alcoholism Substance Abuse and Mental Health Services
Administration, Public Health Service Willco Bldg., Suite 400-MSC7003
6000 Executive Blvd. Bethesda, MD 20892 Tel: 301/443-3851

National Institute on Drug Abuse
Substance Abuse and Mental Health Services Administration, Public Health Service 5600 Fishers Lane, Room 18-49
Rockville, MD 20857
Tel: 301/443-0107

Organizations Providing Information on Drug Courts:

Drug Court Clearinghouse & Technical
Assistance Project
American University
Justice Programs Office
4400 Massachusetts Avenue, NW
Brandywine, Suite 660
Washington, DC 20016-8159
Tel: 202/885-2875
Fax: 202/885-2885

Justice Management Institute
1900 Grant St., Suite 815
Denver, CO 80203 Tel: 303/831-7564 Fax: 303/831-4564
National Association of Drug Court Professionals
901 North Pitt St., Suite 300
Alexandria, VA 22314
Tel: 800/542-2322 or 703/706-0576
Fax: 703/706-0565

National TASC
8630 Fenton St., Suite 121 Silver Spring, MD 20910 Tel: 301/608-0595
Fax: 301/608-0599

State Justice Institute 1650 King St., Suite 600 Alexandria, VA 22314
Tel: 703/684-6100
Fax: 703/684-7618

Private Organizations Providing Information on AOD Treatment:

American Society of Addiction
Medicine, Inc.
Upper Arcade, Suite 101 4601 North Park Avenue Chevy Chase, MD 20815
Tel: 301/656-3920

Guidepoints: Acupuncture in Recovery
(Information on innovative treatment
of addictive and mental disorders) 7402 NE 58th St.
Vancouver, WA 98662
Tel: 360/254-0186

National Acupuncture Detoxification
Association
P.O. Box 1927
Vancouver, WA 98668-1927
Tel and Fax: 360/260-8620

National Association of Alcohol & Drug Abuse Counselors
1911 North Fort Meyer Drive, Suite 900 Arlington, VA 22209
Tel: 703/741-7686

National Association of State Alcohol and
Drug Abuse Directors (NASADAD) 444 North Capitol St., Suite 642
Washington, DC 20001
Tel: 202/783-6868
Fax: 202/783-2704

National GAINS Center for People with Co-occurring Disorders in the Justice System
Policy Research, Inc.
262 Delaware Ave
Delmar, NY 12054
Tel: 800/331-GAIN
Fax: 518/439-7612

Private Organizations Providing Information on Community Anti-Drug Alliances:

Community Anti-Drug Coalitions of America
(CADCA)
James Copple, Executive Director
701 North Fairfax
Alexandria, VA 22314
Tel: 703/706-0563
Drug Strategies, Inc.
2445 M Street, NW, Suite 480
Washington, DC 20037 Tel: 202/663-6090
Join Together
441 Stuart Street, 6th Floor
Boston, MA 02116 Tel: 617/437-1500

Partnership for a Drug Free America
State Alliance Program
405 Lexington Ave., 16th Floor
New York, NY 10174 Tel: 212/922-1560

End Notes

[1] Hubbard, R., Marsden, M., Rachal, J., Harwood, H., Cavanaugh E., and Ginzburg, H. Drug Abuse Treatment: A National Study of Effectiveness. Chapel Hill: University of North Carolina Press, 1989. Pringle G.H., Impact of the criminal justice system on substance abusers seeking professional help, Journal of Drug Issues, Summer, pp. 275–283, vol 12, no. 3, 1982.

[2] All communication about an individual's participation in treatment must be in compliance with the provisions of 42 CFR, Part 2 (the federal regulations governing confidentiality of alcohol and drug abuse patient records), and with similar State and local regulations.

[3] Treatment-Based Drug Court Planning Guide and Checklist, Combining Alcohol and Other Drug Abuse Treatment With Diversion for Juveniles in the Justice System, TIP #21, Treatment Drug Courts: Integrating Substance Abuse Treatment With Legal Case Processing, TIP #23. Rockville, MD: Center for Substance Abuse Treatment, 1996.

[4] The Effectiveness of Treatment for Drug Abusers Under Criminal Justice Supervision. Lipton, D., Washington, DC: National Institute of Justice, Research Report, November 1995.

[5] Rydell, P., Everingham, S. Controlling Cocaine: Supply Versus Demand Programs. Santa Monica, CA: RAND Corporation, Office of National Drug Control Policy, Policy Research Center, 1994.

[6] Field, G. Oregon prison drug treatment programs. In C. Leukefeld and F. Tims (eds.), Drug Abuse Treatment in Prisons and Jails. Research monograph series #108. Rockville, MD: National Institute on Drug Abuse, 1992. Wexler, H., Falkin, G., and Lipton, D. Outcome evaluation of a prison therapeutic community for substance abuse treatment. Criminal Justice and Behavior, 17, pp 71-92, 1990.

[7] Evaluating Recovery Services: The California Drug and Alcohol Treatment Assessment (CALDATA) General Report. Sacramento, CA: California Department of Alcohol and Drug Programs, April 1994.

[8] Ibid.

[9] Societal Outcomes and Cost Savings of Drug and Alcohol Treatment in the State of Oregon. Salem, OR: Office of Alcohol and Drug Abuse Programs, Oregon Department of Human Resources, February 1996.

INDEX

D

E

F

G

H

I

J

L

M

N

O

P

Q

R

U

V

W

Y